Education reform

Education reform

A critical and
post-structural approach

Stephen J. Ball

Open University Press
Buckingham · Philadelphia

Open University Press
Celtic Court
22 Ballmoor
Buckingham
MK18 1XW

and

1900 Frost Road, Suite 101
Bristol, PA 19007, USA

First Published 1994

A catalogue record of this book is available from the British Library

ISBN 0 335 19272 6 (pb) 0 335 19273 4 (hb)

Library of Congress Cataloging-in-Publication Data
Ball, Stephen J.
    Education reform : a critical and post structural approach /
Stephen J. Ball.
        p.   cm.
    Includes bibliographical references and index.
    ISBN 0–335–19273–4   ISBN 0–335–19272–6 (pbk.)
    1. Education and state—Great Britain.   2. Politics and education—
Great Britain.   3. Educational sociology—Great Britain.
4. Educational change—Great Britain.   I. Title.
LC93.G7B34   1994
379.41—dc20   94–12242
                                                                      CIP

Typeset by Graphicraft Typesetters Ltd, Hong Kong
Printed in Great Britain by St Edmundsbury Press Ltd
Bury St Edmunds, Suffolk

Aun aprendo
(Goya)

Contents

Preface

Versions of most of the chapters in this volume have appeared in print previously but all have been revised, most very significantly. Chapter 2 was originally published in *Discourse* (13/2, 1993); Chapter 3 in *Curriculum Studies* (41/2, 1993); Chapter 4 in the *British Journal of Educational Studies* (41/2, 1993); Chapter 5 in Smyth, J. (ed.) (1993); Chapter 6 in Crump, S. (ed.) *School Centred Leadership*, Melbourne, Nelson (1993); Chapter 7 in the *British Journal of Sociology of Education* (14/1, 1993); Chapter 8 was given as a symposium paper at the Annual Meeting of the American Educational Research Association, Atlanta, April 1993 and later appeared in the *Journal of Curriculum and Supervision* (1994).

A lot of friends and colleagues have given help and support in the development of the material presented here; none more so than my research collaborators Richard Bowe and Sharon Gewirtz. Meg Maguire, Alan Cribb, Trinidad Ball, Barry Troyna, John Fitz, Geoff Whitty, David Halpin, Miriam David, Carole Vincent, Anne West, Stephen Crump, Tony Knight, Margaret Brown, John Evans, Chris Shilling, Sara Kelly and my SIPS colleagues at King's also offered important comments and criticisms, all of which I tried to take seriously, and gave their support, for which I am grateful. I am also grateful to John Skelton for his interest in my work. Most important to the completion of the project and to me is Trinidad, who continues to tolerate my preoccupations.

Glossary

Agencies

CPS; Centre for Policy Studies, founded in 1974 after the Conservative election defeat to 'think' radical ideas. Margaret Thatcher and Keith Joseph were co-chairs.

CRE; Campaign for Real Education, was founded in the wake of the suspension (and eventual 'buying out') of headteacher John Honeyford in Bradford. In part the suspension had resulted from the publication of an article by Honeyford, critical of multiculturalism, in *The Salisbury Review* (see under Roger Scruton). Stewart Deuchar is vice-chairman of the CRE.

DES; Department of Education and Science, renamed Department for Education in 1992 with responsibility for Science hived off.

HMI; Her Majesty's Inspectorate, a semi-autonomous 'quality control' unit based in the DES, identified by restorationist critics as part of the 'old' educational establishment and recently reorganized as OFSTED (the Office for Standards in Education).

LEAs; local education authorities, indirectly elected local government committees which until recently had considerable power and influence over local education policy and provision. Since the 1988 Education Reform Act both power and influence have waned considerably and the 1993 Education Act brought about further reductions in LEA powers and responsibilities.

NCC; National Curriculum Council, established by the 1988 Education Reform Act, responsible for advising the Secretary of State on all aspects of the school curriculum, for carrying out research and development and for publishing and disseminating information relating to the curriculum for schools.

SCAA; School Curriculum and Assessment Authority, replaced SEAC and NCC on 1 October 1993, under the Chairmanship of Sir Ron Dearing. The Authority has fifteen members, including John Marks and Anthony O'Hear, two independent school headteachers, a principal of a CTC, one grant-maintained school headteacher and three 'industry' representatives (including the joint Managing Director of Sainsbury's). The remaining numbers are made up by a higher education college principal, an LEA director of education and three LEA school headteachers.

SEAC; Schools Examination and Assessment Council, established by the 1988 Education Reform Act to advise the Secretary of State and promote the new developments in assessment required under the Act.

Actors

Kenneth Baker; Secretary of State for Education 1986–9, architect of the 1988 Education Reform Act, was promoted to Home Secretary.

Kenneth Clarke; Secretary of State for Education 1990–2, also promoted to Home Secretary.

Professor Brian Cox; co-founder of the Black Papers, right-wing, traditionalist critiques of comprehensive and progress education published from 1969 to 1975, was appointed as Chair of the National Curriculum working party on English. Latterly he has been an increasingly vocal critic of NCC and government policies for English teaching.

Sir Ron Dearing; first Chairman of SCAA, began his career as a civil servant and was more recently Chair of the Universities Funding Council.

Professor Anthony Flew; philosopher of education and member of the Education Group of the Centre for Policy Studies, has also written for the neo-liberal Institute of Economic Affairs and the Social Affairs Unit. He is also on the council of the Freedom Association.

Duncan Graham; ex-LEA chief officer and first chairman of the NCC, deposed in 1991 soon after John Major became Prime Minister.

David (Lord) Griffiths; appointed as Chairman of SEAC in 1991, was previously long-time head of Mrs Thatcher's policy unit, and one time chair of CPS.

Philip Halsey; ex-DES senior civil servant and first chairman of SEAC, deposed in 1991 soon after John Major became Prime Minister.

Keith (Lord) Joseph; Secretary of State for Education 1981–6, Conservative neo-liberal intellectual, political guru of Margaret Thatcher in the 1970s.

Sheila Lawlor; deputy director of the CPS and outspoken critic of progressivism and advocate of traditionalism in education.

John MacGregor; Secretary of State for Education 1989–90, became Leader of the House and in 1992 Minister of Transport.

John Major; Conservative Prime Minister 1990–.

Dr John Marebon; Trinity College, Cambridge, husband of Sheila Lawlor and author of CPS pamphlet on English teaching, appointed to SEAC in 1992.

John Marks; member of several right-wing, restorationist groups, including the CPS, National Council for Educational Standards and Hillgate Group, recently a pamphlet writer for the CRE, latterly dubbed as 'government examinations advisor', member of both NCC (since 1992) and SEAC (since 1990). Other right-wingers, or people associated with restorationist issues, have been appointed to NCC and SEAC, including John McIntosh (NCC), John Barnes (SEAC), Dr Anthony Freeman (SEAC) and Martin Turner (SEAC).

Professor Anthony O'Hear; philosopher and CPS pamphlet writer, *Daily Telegraph* columnist, government appointee to the Council for the Accreditation of Teacher Education.

Lady Plowden; Chair of the advisory committee which produced the Plowden Report, a high profile and influential pro-progressive report on primary education published in 1967.

John Patten; Secretary of State for Education 1992–.

David Pascall; executive of British Petroleum, appointed as Chair of NCC in 1991, was a member of Mrs Thatcher's policy unit 1983–4.

Roger Scruton; Professor of Aesthetics at Birkbeck College, editor of the High Tory journal *The Salisbury Review*, and writer for and member of several restorationist groups, including the Educational Research Centre and Institute for European Defence and Strategic Studies.

Margaret Thatcher; Conservative Prime Minister 1979–90.

David Willetts; was Director of Studies of the Centre for Policy Studies, won a safe Conservative seat in the 1992 general election, is author of *Modern Conservativism* (1992).

1

Post-structuralism, ethnography and the critical analysis of education reform

This book is, in part at least, a follow-up to my earlier work on educational politics and policy making in the UK (Ball 1990b). That research-based study was situated firmly inside the educational state and explored the background to the 1988 Education Reform Act. I also began to develop an analysis of the workings of the educational state and the struggles and conflicts enjoined inside the state apparatuses over the definition of what is to count as education. Here I am extending my analysis beyond the limits of the central state to examine some of the 'power networks', discourses and technologies which run through the social body of education: the local state, educational organizations and classrooms. My focus is particularly upon the secondary school. The 1988 Education Reform Act brought into play a new 'economy' of power, 'that is to say, procedures which allowed the effects of power to circulate in a manner at once continuous, uninterrupted, adapted and "individualized" throughout the entire social body' (Rabinow 1986: 61). This economy is invested in, 'runs through', four essential circuits within the education system, the four message systems of education: curriculum, assessment, pedagogy and organization (Ball 1990b: 122). I concentrate in this book primarily on the fourth but touch also upon the others (see Chapter 3 and below). My aim is to theorize educational reform and thereby achieve an 'unmasking of power for those who suffer it' (Sheridan 1980: 221).

Three epistemologies or analytical perspectives fight to be heard in this theory-work. They are employed as interpretive resources in an exercise in 'applied sociology'. At times they clash and grate against one another but the resultant friction is, I hope, purposeful and effective rather than a distraction. They are: critical policy analysis, post-structuralism and critical ethnography. Regarding the first, John Prunty explains:

> The personal values and political commitment of the critical policy analyst would be anchored in the vision of a moral order in which justice, equality and individual freedom are uncompromised by the avarice of a few. The critical analyst would endorse political, social and economic arrangements where persons are never treated as a means to an end, but treated as ends in their own right.
>
> (Prunty 1985: 136)

And, as Harvey (1990: 8) points out, critical social research is 'not bounded by a single (grand) theoretical perspective. It is not (a version of) Marxism, or feminism, or anything else for that matter' (see Troyna 1993). The critical analyst must take risks, use imagination, but also be reflexive. The concern is with the task rather than with theoretical purism or conceptual niceties. But some modesty is also required, a willing uncertainty and a reluctance to leap to analytical closure. The task, then, is to examine the moral order of reform and the relationship of reform to existing patterns of social inequality, bringing to bear those concepts and interpretive devices which offer the best possibilities of insight and understanding.

Second, the emphasis in post-structural analysis is on the discourses and texts which come into play in the make-up of social institutions and cultural products. Post-structuralism offers very different ways of looking at and beyond the obvious and puts different sorts of questions on the agenda for change. 'Discourse transmits and produces power; it reinforces it, but also undermines and exposes it, renders it fragile and makes it possible to thwart it' (Foucault 1981: 101). Discourses partake of power and knowledge; that is to say, power and knowledge are fused in the practices that comprise history.

Third, I draw on the methods, data and analytical procedures of ethnography, in order to generate critical perspectives upon the impact and effects of policy in local settings. Ethnography provides access to 'situated' discourses and 'specific tactics' and 'precise and tenuous' power relations operating in local settings (see Chapter 5). Ethnography is also a counterpoint to the bland and misleading, rational scientism (or psycho-humanism) which predominates within the more prescriptive writing of educational management and administration. And it offers a way of bringing into play the concerns and interests and diverse voices of marginalized or oppressed social groups; as well as a way of accessing the voices of authority and influence (Gewirtz and Ozga 1990). This was central to the US Chicago tradition, and in the UK, particularly since the work of Willis (1976), educational ethnography has been oriented to the exploration and documentation of 'resistance' and the interplay of domination and struggle. Thomas (1993: vii) defines critical ethnography as:

> a way of applying a subversive worldview to the conventional logic of cultural inquiry. It does not stand in opposition to conventional ethnography. Rather, it offers a more direct style of thinking about relationships among knowledge, society and political action. The central premise is that one can be both scientific and critical, and that ethnographic description offers a powerful means of critiquing culture and the role of research within it.

Now for any thoroughgoing Foucauldian there would undoubtedly be a number of problems with this last statement. However, I see a possible role for ethnography (as sets of cultural texts) in relation to theorization, similar to the role played by historical texts in Foucault's genealogical method. In other words, there is a methodological affinity between ethnography and genealogy. (There are also important parallels between critical policy research and Foucauldian sociology.) Foucault defines genealogy as:

> the union of erudite and local memories which allows us to establish a historical knowledge of struggles and to make use of this knowledge tactically today ... What it really does is to entertain the claims to attention of local, discontinuous, disqualified, illegitimate knowledge against the claims of a unitary body of theory that would filter, hierarchise, and order them in the name of some true knowledge.
>
> (Foucault 1980: 83)

The genealogical approach interrupts the taken-for-granted and isolates the contingent power relations which make it possible for particular assertions to operate as absolute truths. It does so, in part, by providing a conduit for submerged voices which are obscured and marginalized by specific power–knowledge arrangements (Sawicki 1991: 28). It enables an 'insurrection of subjugated knowledges' (Foucault 1980: 81). In effect, genealogy identifies and counterpoints antagonistic discourses – the dominant and the silenced, the 'truthful' and illegitimate.

Ethnography is a way of engaging critically with, and developing interpretations of, 'the real'. Like genealogy it is disruptive, it is often about giving voice to the unheard, it is also about the play of power–knowledge relations in local and specific settings; here, the curriculum, management, leadership, choice and competition. It enables the analyst to focus upon and explore 'events', spaces which divide those in struggle. It is very much about local memories and marginalized perspectives (Maguire and Ball 1994). As Thomas (1993: 68) argues, 'Critical thinking that challenges accepted images and tweaks the conscience into intellectual re-examination and social action embodies a struggle over ideas, metaphors, policies and behaviour.' But there is no attempt to construct a thoroughgoing ethnography of reform here. The quotations from empirical data are for the illustration and analysis of discourses and 'events'. Most are taken from an ESRC-funded study of market forces in secondary education, part of which is based upon longitudinal case studies of 16 schools (ESRC grant no. 232858).

These, then, are my tools. I intend to apply them as best I can to some aspects of current educational reform. I recognize that I am straddling, somewhat uncomfortably, a crucial epistemological divide in trying to marry and use these different perspectives (see Jones and Ball 1994). I am also not unwilling to admit my ambivalence about certain versions of post-structuralism, to own up to a modernist commitment to the idea of 'the real' and to the constraints of the material context or to wanting to retain some version of purposive agency (see Chapter 2). But I am also clear that modernist sociology cannot ignore either the epistemological challenge or analytical insights presented by post-structuralism. As a final stage in preparatory ground-clearing I want to sketch in some of the general discursive terrain into which the individual analytical pieces which follow fit.

The contradictions of reform

A set of basic tensions are embedded in the Conservative educational state (reflecting and reproducing more general state problems). These drive and inform policies and produce tensions and incoherences within policy making. The problems of the state are both structural *and* played out in micropolitical struggles inside the state itself. There are three 'fields' of problems: (a) the problem of capital accumulation and economic efficiency; (b) the problem of social order, social authority and stability; and (c) the technical and managerial problems of the state itself – governance and control (legal and administrative procedures), costs (public spending) and planning. At any point in time these problems are informed by and inscribed within particular political discourses. Some of the main thrusts of recent education policy can be related back to or understood in terms of these generic problems. I shall begin by taking the National Curriculum as a case in point.

The vocational emphasis within education policy through the mid-1980s and represented (weakly) at least in the initial 1988 version of the National Curriculum, the Mark 1 National Curriculum (Mk1C) (Ball 1994), was certainly intended to inflect the curriculum, assessment and pedagogy towards the changing needs of post-Fordist industrial production (and thus enhance national economic performance). The orientation of new developments in teaching and learning in science and mathematics in particular had strong affinities with the development of flexible production methods in industry. The challenge of 'progressive vocationalism' (Ball 1990b) to textual authority, the traditional role of the teacher and formalist conceptions of knowledge presented an extraordinary and, as it turned out, short-lived moment for progressive educational reform. It serves to point up very dramatically the inherent contradictions between the economic and the political within state policy making. From 1990 on National Curriculum planning has taken a different turn; this is what might be termed the Mark 2 National Curriculum (Mk2C), driven by what I term 'cultural restorationism' (see Chapter 3), and rooted in an agenda of state problems related to social order and legitimation.

In particular, neo-conservative cultural restorationism ties together education, the family and the state with the past. The national language and national identity play a key role in this (Ball *et al.* 1990). As Aronowitz and Giroux (1991: 42) comment, writing about US restorationist Hirsch, 'the national language, which is at the centre of his notion of literacy, is rooted in a civic religion that forms the core of stability in the culture itself.' Thus, in the UK the English curriculum is crucial terrain in the culture wars. Via struggles to control the form of the language and to set firm boundaries around the definition of the literary canon, markers of national and ethnic identity and a basis for moral and social regulation are established. 'For language lies at the root of human identity, and to tamper with that is either poetry or treason' (Eagleton 1993: 35). And 'literature . . . is the concrete correlate of that abstract political unity which we share as formally equal citizens of the state' (Eagleton 1993: 32). The Mk1C and more profoundly and blatantly the Mk2C are attempts to recreate magically a mythical past of English cultural unity. Ethnic and cultural diversity are made invisible by the recomposition of Englishness within the National Curriculum. An imaginary past of national glories and civilizing influence is to serve as model and guardian for the future. 'The neo-conservatives see their role, on the one hand, in the mobilization of pasts which can be accepted approvingly and, on the other, in the neutralization of those pasts which would provoke only criticism and rejection' (Habermas 1985: 91). Culture is made over into an artefact, history becomes a 'museum of information' (Aronowitz and Giroux 1991). 'We are dealing here with ideologues for whom language is essentially an elocutionary affair, poetry a kind of metrical patriotism, and English literature a semantic Stonehenge' (Eagleton 1993: 35). In Bernstein's terms the National Curriculum establishes a set of decisive 'insulations':

> punctuations written by power relations that establish as the order of things distinct subjects through distinct voices. Indeed, insulation is the means whereby the cultural is transformed into the natural, the contingent into the necessary, the past into the present, the present into the future.
>
> (Bernstein 1990: 25)

(An analogous set of insulations is employed in the increasingly fine definitions of Britishness enacted through immigration legislation.) A new category of Englishness is thus forged, or at least attempted, through the media of speech, grammar and literature. 'Imaginary subjects' are created, 'whose voices are experienced as real, as validating and constituting the specialized category' (Bernstein 1990: 25). Here the 'voice' is both metaphorical and eminently real. The breaks and dislocations which the Mk2C seeks to establish insulate literary from popular culture, received from demotic pronunciation, 'proper' language from language 'in use', national identity from origin and ethnicity, history from politics, and social consciousness from social experience (see Chapter 3). The objective here is 'de-pluralization'; the articulation of a classless and monoethnic society with a common, transcendent culture.

Let me be clear, the shift I am trying to identify here is a relative one. The Mk1C was already established upon conservative and traditionalist principles in many respects. It was already subject to criticism from representatives of industry suspicious of its regressive structure. 'They are concerned that he [Secretary of State, Kenneth Baker] has given "too much importance to narrow academic knowledge and too little to the fostering of transferable skills and learning ability" ' (Jackson 1989; quoted in Whitty 1990: 29). As I see it the Mk1C was a kind of political compromise, although a compromise unstably founded on terms set by the Conservative government. Each subject in turn was struggled over in private (see Ball 1990b) and debated in public. The Mk2C is much more uncompromising, much more a curriculum by fiat, an authoritarian curriculum (although some private struggles continue). The shift might be seen as the latest stages in what I have described as a 'series of ratchet steps, each one based upon a firmer, more clearly defined and more clearly determined curriculum. Attempts are made to mobilise acceptance at each turn of the ratchet – a process of climate building' (Ball 1990b: 147). Each turn relates to a change in what is politically possible.

How can we begin to explain the resurgence of traditional forms of curriculum practice which appear to be divorced from and antithetical to the requirements of capital accumulation, during a time of international recession when the state of industry and the economy occupy the centre ground of politics?[1] Interestingly, Aronowitz and Giroux (1991: 24) note a similar policy turn in the USA, in Reagan's second presidential term: 'The importance of linking educational reform to the needs of big business has continued to influence the debate, while demands that schools provide the skills necessary for domestic production and expanding capital abroad have slowly given way to an overriding emphasis on schools as sites of cultural production.' This suggests that generic political, rather than economic, causes may underlie the shift towards 'cultural rightism'. (However, the relationship between education and the economy can be construed in a variety of ways. Former Secretary of State Kenneth Baker had more than a passing interest in Japanese education, which stresses national pride/identity and uniformity rather than vocationalism (Maguire 1993).)

Bernstein's account of the principles of social control in education provides a useful starting point for the interpretation of curriculum policy, although the National Curriculum signals a shift in
the opposite direction to the one he is concerned with; that is, from
a relatively integrated to a collection code. This is a refreezing of
boundaries, a response to a crisis in power and control.

> I suggest that the movement away from collection to integrated
> codes symbolizes that there is a crisis in society's basic classifi-
> cations and frames, and therefore a crisis in its structures of
> power and principles of control. The movement from this point
> of view represents an attempt to declassify and so alter power
> structures and principles of control; in doing so to unfreeze
> the structuring of knowledge and to change the boundaries of
> consciousness. From this point of view integrated codes are
> symptoms of moral crisis rather than a terminal state of an
> education system.
>
> (Bernstein 1971: 67)

Bernstein's *crisis* in effect points up a fundamental contradiction
within education and in the relationship of education to the modern
state and the modern economy. The integration of education and
work, while serving the requirements of capital accumulation, threatens (or at least fails to concern itself with the reproduction of) the
established social order and fails to achieve the requirements of
social authority and the legitimation of hierarchy and differentiation. For the cultural restorationists (or neo-conservatives as they are
also called) education has become implicated in what Habermas
(1985: 80) describes as 'the so-called *inflation of expectations* and *the
lack of willingness to acclaim and obey*, which is based on tradition.' And
again this is articulated in the language of *crisis*: 'The current crisis
is above all a cultural crisis . . . The problem is that our convictions
are full of holes, our morals and our manners corrupt' (Steinfels
1979: 55). Writing of the US education system, Aronowitz and Giroux
(1991) describe a similar restorationist impetus as militating around
a '*cultural crisis*' in education.

What I have called vocational/new progressivism in education is
an aspect of, in Habermas's terms, social modernism. While such
social modernism is not unwelcome in itself to the cultural restorationists, its apparently inevitable association with cultural modernity

– the changing boundaries of consciousness – is most certainly unacceptable.[2]

> Danger lies in cultural transformations, motivational and atti-
> tudinal changes and shifts in patterns of values and identities,
> which are attributed to the entry of cultural innovations into
> more or less traditional forms of life. Therefore, the legacy of
> tradition has to be preserved as far as possible.
>
> (Habermas 1985: 87)

What Habermas calls 'the programmatic dismissal of cultural modernity', which 'should make room for a *healthy sense of tradition*'
(p. 91), captures the essential features of the Mk2C perfectly.

> It concentrates on a 'courage to educate', i.e., an educational
> policy which tailors elementary education to basic skills and
> secondary virtues (industriousness, discipline and cleanliness).
> Simultaneously it emphasises a 'courage of the past' in schools,
> the family and the state.
>
> (Habermas 1985: 91)

The 'courage of the past' is evident in a second and different
thrust of contemporary education policy: the attempt to 'roll back
the state' and recreate a version of the *laissez-faire* politics of the early
and mid-nineteenth century by inserting the market form into areas
of health, education and social service which had previously been
planned and delivered, centrally or locally, by state agencies. As
pointed out by numerous commentators, there is more than a little
contradiction between the centralizing tendencies of the National
Curriculum and the decentralizing of school budgets and organizational control, through the LMS (local management of schools)
initiative, and the introduction of market discipline via parental
choice. There are, however, ways of resolving this contradiction which
render the various aspects of policy as 'of a piece'. Whitty (1989:
331) argues, for example, that 'there may actually be an ideological
congruity rather than incongruity between the national curriculum
proposals and other aspects of the Education Reform Act.' He suggests
that

> Schools which are responsive to choices made by parents in the
> market are believed by the government to be more likely than
> those administered by state bureaucrats to produce high levels

of scholastic achievement, to benefit both individuals and the nation. The strength of the state therefore has to be used to remove anything that interferes with this process or with the development of an appropriate sense of self and the nation on the part of citizens who will be making their choice in the market.

(Whitty 1989: 331)

However, one of the points I argue in the later chapters (3, 4, 5 and 6) is that the autonomy of schools is more apparent than real. There may be no real contradiction after all. The use of performativity and target-related funding as a form of control, linked to the localized, productive and capillary power of 'the manager', presents a solution to the problems of 'ungovernability'; that is, government overload, which allows the state to retain considerable 'steerage' over the goals and processes of the education system (while appearing not to do so). Indeed, the market form offers a powerful response to a whole set of technical, managerial and ideological problems. It appears to give greater power to all parents, while systematically advantaging some and disadvantaging others, and effectively reproducing the classic lines of the social and technical division of labour. It plays its part in the reformulation of citizenship, as the mode of consumption is generalized (Bowe *et al.* 1994b). And it serves to generalize further the commodity form, a basic ideological building brick of capitalist culture and subjectivity. The emphasis on individualized and priva- tized family life is ramified, and the collectivist orientation weakly articulated within comprehensive education is sidelined (see Chap- ter 8). Education is steadily being incorporated into the 'shopping mall society' (Shields 1992).

Beyond the state

Any decent theory of education policy must attend to the workings of the state. But any decent theory of education policy must not be limited to a state control perspective. Policy is, as already indicated, an 'economy of power', a set of technologies and practices which are realized and struggled over in local settings. Policy is both text and action, words and deeds, it is what is enacted as well as what is intended (see Chapter 2). Policies are always incomplete insofar as they relate to or map on to the 'wild profusion' of local practice. Policies are crude and simple. Practice is sophisticated, contingent, complex and unstable. Policy *as* practice is 'created' in a trialectic of dominance, resistance and chaos/freedom. Thus, policy is no simple asymmetry of power: 'Control [or dominance] can never be totally secured, in part because of agency. It will be open to erosion and undercutting by the action, embodied agency of those people who are its object' (Clegg 1989: 193). Thus, we need to go beyond the dominance/resistance binary (Scheurich 1992), not to erase it but to extend it. To paraphrase Scheurich, much of practice occurs outside of the confines of the dominance/resistance binary. There is just more to school and classroom life than this, a third space – other concerns, demands, pressures, purposes and desires.

In putting this argument I do not intend to minimize or underestimate the effects or impact of policy; rather I hope to problematize them. Indeed, underestimation would be difficult. Schools in the UK are currently faced with a reform package which includes not only a new national curriculum but also changes in school governance, management and funding, in the roles of local authorities, in student testing and school inspection, in pedagogy and classroom organization (like the press for more whole-class teaching), and in teacher training and teachers' conditions of work and employment. It is easier to capture the scope of change involved by listing those things that remain the same – but A-level examinations may be the only example. These changes are all facets of current Conservative government education policy – they are all externally imposed and virtually all have legal status. They are all happening at once. They all have dramatically short time scales for implementation. By general consensus, within the educational community they are all massively under-funded (Coopers and Lybrand Deloitte 1992). Furthermore, the changes are frequently altered, amended and reoriented, often by ministerial fiat. Advisory committees are set up and then ignored. Development work is commissioned and then cancelled. Teacher representatives are excluded from consultations, consultation processes are deliberately short and responses are typically also ignored. Separately and together these changes are bringing about profound shifts in the nature of teaching and the teachers' role, profound shifts in the relationships between schools and parents and profound shifts in the nature of schools as work organizations. Not surprisingly, many teachers appear weary and wary, stressed and depressed, alienated and bitter. They are faced with threats to their autonomy and status, and livelihood in some cases, but are expected to respond constructively and intelligently to make sense of the uncertainties, incoherence and complexity of change. And in a sense the more successful they are at coping, the more of themselves as professionals and their experience they must forgo; although, for some, the classroom may still be a black box within which they can hide from the currents of reform. Together these changes assert a massive and complex technology of control over teachers' work in all its aspects.

These changes are also tied together in complex ways. They inter-relate and ramify in certain respects (some of which are indicated below) but they also contradict and confuse in various ways. In Cuban's terms both first-order, quality control, and second-order, design, reforms are in train. And there is no evidence in either respect of the modesty on the part of reformers which he calls for (Cuban 1990). Clearly, inside the school and classroom practice, it is school managers and classroom teachers who must put the bits and pieces together – construct their own subjection if you like. Individually and collectively they must make sense of reform, and at organization and classroom level develop interpretations and prac-tices which engage seriously with the changes and their consequences for working relationships and for teaching and learning. It is with the middle level, the organization and institution of 'the school' and the meaning and practice of 'the teacher', that this book is primarily concerned; that is, the local contexts, realizations and displacements of policy.

Chapter 2 develops further the theorization of policy which was begun here. Chapter 3 explores the discursive project of the cultural restorationist version of the National Curriculum. Chapter 4 considers the ways in which recent policy changes in curriculum, school management and local relations between schools have begun a sig-nificant reworking of the meaning of 'the teacher'. Chapter 5 takes the concern with management further by a critical analysis of the idea of 'self-managing school'. Chapters 4 and 5 draw in particular on Foucault's work on power and moral technologies. Chapter 6 is written from a more realist stance and uses data from research in a variety of schools to examine the uncertainties of and changes in modes of school leadership. Chapters 7 and 8 are about the educa-tion market. Chapter 7 presents a wide-ranging critique of choice theory and Chapter 8 considers the values, changes and ethical di-lemmas with which the market form confronts heads of schools.

Notes

1 Writing in 1993, the centre ground of politics is as much about the social as the economic. Rising crime figures, juvenile and child crime, crimes against the police and social unrest in areas of economic distress have begun to generate a reactive discourse of public morals which makes the current politics of school and family much less surprising than I am perhaps presenting it in the main text. The tensions between Thatcherist competitive individualism and the concern with the decline of moral identity and the decline of deference have never been so clear-cut as now (Minogue 1993). Guilt, shame and virtue do not sit easily alongside challenge, initiative and self-interest. This is pointed up by recent interventions in the moral panic over juvenile criminality by Prime Minister, John Major, and Archbishop of York, John Habgood. The former had called for society 'to condemn a little more and understand a little less'. The latter retaliated, arguing that 'The Government, with its strong emphasis on competitive success, feeds the notion that in our society, in a sense, we are against each other and one does need some countervailing forces to show that actually true human life is about cooperation ... I am not saying that people aren't bad but often badness is brought out of them by circumstances, by upbringing, by the sense of boredom and a by a sense of hopelessness.'

2 Even the commitment of UK Conservatives to social modernity can be questioned. The politics and organization of the National Curriculum, for example, are primarily Taylorist rather than post-Fordist. There is little evidence of attempts to achieve negotiated consent from, or *Kalmarist* autonomy for, teachers. Rather, schools and teachers are caught between the raw disciplines of market and state.

2

What is policy? Texts, trajectories
and toolboxes

This chapter is an exercise in theoretical heurism. It is intentionally
tentative and open-ended. I realize that on occasion I resort to
aphorism rather than argument. It rests in part on an oddly unfash-
ionable position in educational and sociological research; that is,
that in the analysis of complex social issues – like policy – two theories are probably better than one. To put it another way, the *complexity*
and *scope* of policy analysis – from an interest in the workings of the
state to a concern with contexts of practice and the distributional
outcomes of policy – precludes the possibility of successful single-
theory explanations. What we need in policy analysis is a toolbox of
diverse concepts and theories – an applied sociology rather than a
pure one. Thus, I want to replace the modernist theoretical project
of abstract parsimony with a somewhat more post-modernist one of
localized complexity. This polarization, between parsimony and
complexity, and the dilemmas it highlights are very much to the fore
in recent debates in the UK about the conception and purposes of
'policy-sociology' (Ozga 1987, 1990; Ball 1990b). Thus, Ozga (1990:
359) suggests that it is important to 'bring together structural, macro-
level analysis of education systems and education policies and micro-
level investigation, especially that which takes account of people's
perception and experiences.' Now that is what I mean by scope
and I agree strongly with Ozga's plea. But she goes on to criticize
approaches that generate 'a view of policy making which stresses ad
hocery, serendipity, muddle and negotiation' (p. 360). Now that is
part of what I mean by complexity (or at least one aspect of it) and
I disagree with the exclusory thrust of Ozga's plea. We cannot rule

out certain forms and conceptions of social action simply because they seem awkward, theoretically challenging or difficult. The challenge is to relate together analytically the ad hocery of the macro with the ad hocery of the micro without losing sight of the systematic bases and effects of *ad hoc* social actions: to look for the iterations embedded within chaos. As I see it, this also involves some rethinking of the simplicities of the structure/agency dichotomy. This task is one which Harker and May (1993: 177) identify as central to Bourdieu's sociology; that is, 'to account for agency in a constrained world, and show how agency and structure are implicit in each other, rather than being the two poles of a continuum'.

One of the conceptual problems currently lurking within much policy research and policy sociology is that more often than not analysts fail to define conceptually what they mean by policy. The meaning of policy is taken for granted and theoretical and epistemological dry rot is built into the analytical structures they construct. It is not difficult to find the term policy being used to describe very different 'things' at different points in the same study. For me, much rests on the meaning or possible meanings that we give to policy; it affects 'how' we research and how we interpret what we find. Now let me add quickly that I do not exempt myself from these criticisms, although in recent work with Richard Bowe we have tried to be careful and explicit about our understanding and use of the term policy (Bowe and Ball with Gold 1992; see also Chapter 1).

Typically in a piece of writing which begins like this one I would now offer my own definitive version of the meaning of policy, and with a few rhetorical flourishes and a bit of fancy theoretical footwork I would solve all the problems that I have pointed up. But I cannot do that. Or at least I cannot do that very simply. The reason is that I hold my own theoretical uncertainties about the meaning of policy and in current writing on policy issues I actually inhabit two very different conceptualizations of policy. For the time being I will call these *policy as text* and *policy as discourse*. In simple terms the differences between these two conceptualizations are rather dramatic and in sociological terms rather hoary and traditional. But the point I am moving on to is that policy is not one or the other, but both: they are 'implicit in each other'. As an aside, but an important aside, the question 'what is policy?' should not mislead us into unexamined assumptions about policies as 'things'; policies are also processes and outcomes (more of which later).

Policy as text

Here, somewhat under the influence of literary theory, we can see
policies as representations which are encoded in complex ways (via
struggles, compromises, authoritative public interpretations and
reinterpretations) and decoded in complex ways (via actors' interpretations and meanings in relation to their history, experiences,
skills, resources and context). A policy is both contested and changing, always in a state of 'becoming', of 'was' and 'never was' and 'not
quite'; 'for any text a plurality of readers must necessarily produce
a plurality of readings' (Codd 1988: 239). Now this conception is not
simply one which privileges the significance of readings of policy by
its subjects. While that is important – authors cannot control the
meanings of their texts – policy authors do make concerted efforts
to assert such control by the means at their disposal, to achieve
a 'correct' reading. We need to understand those efforts and their
effects on readers and to recognize the attention that readers pay to
the writers' context of production and communicative intent (Giddens
1987: 105–7). But, in addition, it is crucial to recognize that the policies themselves, the texts, are not necessarily clear or closed or complete. The texts are the product of compromises at various stages
(at points of initial influence, in the micropolitics of legislative formulation, in the parliamentary process and in the politics and
micropolitics of interest group articulation). They are typically the
cannibalized products of multiple (but circumscribed) influences
and agendas. There is ad hocery, negotiation and serendipity within
the state, within the policy formulation process.

Now if this sounds like a restatement of the epistemology of pluralism it is not meant to be. There is a difference between agenda
control and ideological politics and the processes of policy influence
and text production within the state. Only certain influences and
agendas are recognized as legitimate, only certain voices are heard
at any point in time. The point is that quibbling and dissensus still
occur with the babble of 'legitimate' voices and sometimes the effects
of quibbling and dissensus result in a blurring of meanings within
texts, and in public confusion and a dissemination of doubt. We only
have to look at Edwards *et al.*'s (1989, 1992) studies of the assisted
places scheme and city technology colleges to see that sometimes it
is actually difficult even to identify analytically what a policy is and
what it is intended to achieve. These studies also point up a second

issue. Policies shift and change their meaning in the arenas of politics; representations change, key interpreters (secretaries of state, ministers, chairs of councils) change (sometimes the change in key actors is a deliberate tactic for changing the meaning of policy). Policies have their own momentum inside the state; purposes and intentions are reworked and reoriented over time. The problems faced by the state change over time. Policies are represented differently by different actors and interests: Kenneth Baker's grant maintained schools scheme as against Margaret Thatcher's; Margaret Thatcher's National Curriculum as against John Major's, Kenneth Baker's, Kenneth Clarke's and Ron Dearing's. At all stages in the policy process we are confronted both with different interpretations of policy, and with what Rizvi and Kemmis (1987) call 'interpretations of interpretations'. And these attempts to represent or rerepresent policy sediment and build up over time; they spread confusion and allow for play in and the playing off of meanings. Gaps and spaces for action and response are opened up or reopened as a result. Thus, the physical text that pops through the school letterbox, or wherever, does not arrive 'out of the blue' – it has an interpretational and representational history – and neither does it enter a social or institutional vacuum. The text and its readers and the context of response all have histories. Policies enter existing patterns of inequality, e.g. the structure of local markets, local class relations. They 'impact' or are taken up differently as a result (see Ball *et al.* (1993a) on the middle-class use of local education markets). Policy is not exterior to inequalities, although it may change them; it is also affected, inflected and deflected by them.

Some texts are never even read firsthand. An ongoing study of the maths National Curriculum has found that 7 per cent of its sample of maths teachers have never read any National Curriculum documents (Brown 1992); an ongoing study of assessment at Key Stage 1 finds that a significant number of teachers in the 32 case study schools fundamentally misunderstand the premises and methods of School Attainment Tasks and teacher assessment and have employed these misunderstandings to organize their classroom practice (Gipps and Brown 1992). Confusion begets confusion. But there may often be key mediators of policy in any setting who are relied upon by others to relate policy to context or to gatekeep, e.g. headteachers (Wallace 1988) or heads of department (Bowe and Ball with Gold 1992). And certain policy texts may be collectively undermined (e.g. the 1993

teacher unions' stand against national testing for 14-year-olds and
the publications of school test results for 7- and 14-year-olds) or
may generate mass confusion and demoralization. Pollard (1992:
112) provides a very good example of both the mediation and
delegitimation of a text: the Schools Examination and Assessment
Council *Guide to Teacher Assessment* (1990).

> This document, which was intended to provide INSET support
> to schools, seriously failed to connect with primary teachers'
> views about learning or with the practicalities of the circum-
> stances in which they work. For instance, it was suggested that
> 'lessons' are planned with direct reference to Attainment Targets
> and suggested, unproblematically, that the National Curriculum
> has set out the order in which children would learn. To teachers
> and advisers who retained child-centred beliefs and an aware-
> ness of the diverse patterns by which children learn, this was
> like a red rag to a bull. There was also enormous hilarity and
> anger over the impracticality of many of the suggestions which
> were made. In particular, the authors of the materials seemed
> to have no awareness of the demands of teaching with large
> class sizes and made a number of simplistic and naive sugges-
> tions. The credibility of the document was thus heavily under-
> cut. SEAC was then humiliated by an article on the materials by
> Ted Wragg in *The Times Educational Supplement* entitled 'Who
> put the "Ass" in Assessment?' and a large number of schools
> and LEAs actively discouraged the circulation or use of the
> *Guide.*

None the less, policies *are* textual interventions into practice; and
although many teachers (and others) are proactive, 'writerly', readers
of texts, their readings and reactions are not constructed in circumstances of their own making. Policies pose problems to their
subjects, problems that must be solved in context. It may be possible
for some to 'hide' from policy but that is rarely a common option.
I must be very clear, policy 'matters: it is important, not the least
because it consists of texts which are (sometimes) *acted on*' (Beilharz
1987: 394). The point is that we cannot predict or assume how they
will be acted on in every case in every setting, or what their immediate
effect will be, or what room for manoeuvre actors will find for themselves. Action may be constrained differently (even tightly) but it is
not determined by policy. Solutions to the problems posed by policy

texts will be localized and should be expected to display ad hocery and messiness. Responses must be 'creative'; but I use the term carefully here and in a specific sense. Given constraints, circumstances and practicalities, the translation of the crude, abstract simplicities of policy texts into interactive and sustainable practices of some sort involves productive thought, invention and adaptation. Policies do not normally tell you what to do, they create circumstances in which the range of options available in deciding what to do are narrowed or changed, or particular goals or outcomes are set. A response must still be put together, constructed in context, offset against other expectations. All of this involves creative social action, not robotic reactivity. Thus, the enactment of texts relies on things like commitment, understanding, capability, resources, practical limitations, cooperation and (importantly) intertextual compatibility. Furthermore, sometimes when we focus analytically on one policy or one text we forget that other policies and texts are in circulation, and the enactment of one may inhibit or contradict or influence the possibility of the enactment of others (I could illustrate most of these points with data from our Education Reform Act study; Bowe and Ball with Gold 1992). And the more ideologically abstract any policy is, the more distant in conception from practice (as in the example above), the less likely it is to be accommodated in unmediated form into the context of practice; it confronts 'other realities', other circumstances, like poverty, disrupted classrooms, lack of materials, multilingual classes. Some policies change some of the circumstances in which we work; they cannot change all the circumstances. Riseborough (1992), in a detailed analysis of the policy responses of one primary headteacher, draws our attention to the importance of 'secondary adjustments' in teachers' engagement with policy: 'teachers can create, through a repertoire of individual and collective, "contained" (i.e. "fitting in without introducing pressure for radical change") and "disruptive" (i.e. attempts to radically alter the structure or leave) strategies, an empirically rich underlife to policy intention' (p. 37). Generally, we have failed to research, analyse and conceptualize this underlife, the 'secondary adjustments' which relate teachers to policy and to the state in different ways. We tend to begin by assuming the adjustment of teachers and context to policy but not of policy to context (see Chapter 1). There is a privileging of the policy maker's reality. The crude and over-used term 'resistance' is a poor substitute here, which allows for both

rampant over-claims and dismissive under-claims to be made about
the way policy problems are solved in context. I also want to avoid
the notion that policy is always negatively responded to, or that all
policies are coercive or regressive. Some emancipatory policies are
subject to creative non-implementation (education history is littered
with examples). And some policies may be deployed in the context
of practice to displace or marginalize others (see Troyna 1992).

In all this discussion of interpretation and creativity I am not trying
to exclude power. Textual interventions can change things significantly, but I am suggesting that we should not ignore the way that
things stay the same or the ways in which changes are different in
different settings and different from the intentions of policy authors
(where these are clear). Power, as Foucault points out, is productive:
'relations of power are not in superstructural positions, with merely
a role of prohibition or accompaniment; they have a directly productive role, wherever they come into play' (Foucault 1981: 94).
Policies typically posit a restructuring, redistribution and disruption
of power relations, so that different people can and cannot do
different things; again 'relations of power are not in a position of
exteriority with respect to other types of relationships (economic
processes, knowledge relationships, sexual relations), but are are
immanent in the latter' (Foucault 1981: 94). Power is multiplicitous,
overlain, interactive and complex, policy texts *enter* rather than
simply change power relations: hence, again, the complexity of the
relationship between policy intentions, texts, interpretations and
reactions. From a rather different theoretical starting point Offe
(1984: 106) offers a similar view:

> the real social effects ('impact') of a law or institutional service
> are not determined by the wording of laws and statutes ('policy
> output'), but instead are generated primarily as a consequence
> of social disputes and conflicts, for which state policy merely
> establishes the location and timing of the contest, its subject
> matter and 'the rules of the game'. In these cases of extra-
> political or 'external' implementation of social policy measures
> state social policy in no way establishes concrete 'conditions'
> (for example, the level of services, specific insurance against
> difficult living conditions). Instead, it defines the substance of
> conflict and, by differentially empowering or dis-empowering
> the relevant social groups, biases the extent of the specific
> 'utility' of the institutions of social policy for these groups.

What Offe is saying, I think, is that practice and the 'effects' of policy cannot be simply read off from texts and are the outcome of conflict and struggle between 'interests' in context. (The use of the market form within policy and the relative advantage that this allows middle class families to achieve is a case in point; see Chapter 7.)

Thus, I take it as axiomatic that there is agency and there is constraint in relation to policy – this is not a sum-zero game. Policy analysis requires an understanding that is based not on constraint *or* agency but on the changing relationships between constraint *and* agency and their inter-penetration. Furthermore, such an analysis must achieve insight into both overall and localized outcomes of policy.

But I also want to use this quotation as a transition point in order to move on to the *other* things I want to say about policy. First, I want to take up the point made that state policy 'establishes the location and timing of the contest, its subject matter and "the rules of the game".' This, I think, highlights the importance of policy *as* and *in* discourse. Second, I want to return to the problem of the 'effects' of policy.

Policy as discourse

In the above there is plenty of social agency and social intentionality around. Actors are making meaning, being influential, contesting, constructing responses, dealing with contradictions, attempting representations of policy. Much of this stuff of policy can be engaged with by a realist analysis in the different contexts of policy. But perhaps this *is* a new pluralism. Perhaps this *is* caught within an ideology of agency; by dealing with what is or can be done it misses what Ozga calls 'the bigger picture'. In other words, perhaps it concentrates too much on what those who inhabit policy think about and misses and fails to attend to what they do not think about. Thus we need to appreciate the way in which policy ensembles, collections of related policies, exercise power through a *production* of 'truth' and 'knowledge', as discourses. Discourses are 'practices that systematically form the objects of which they speak . . . Discourses are not about objects; they do not identify objects, they constitute them and in the practice of doing so conceal their own invention' (Foucault 1977: 49). Discourses are about what can be said, and thought, but also about who can speak, when, where and with what authority. Discourses embody the meaning and use of propositions and words. Thus, certain possibilities for thought are constructed. Words are ordered and combined in particular ways and other combinations are displaced or excluded. 'Discourse may seem of little account', Foucault (1971: 11–12) says, 'but the prohibitions to which it is subject reveal soon enough its links with desire and power.' But discourse is 'irreducible to language and to speech' (Foucault 1974: 49), it is 'more' than that. We do not speak a discourse, it speaks us. *We are* the subjectivities, the voices, the knowledge, the power relations that a discourse constructs and allows. We do not 'know' what we say, we 'are' what we say and do. In these terms we are spoken by policies, we take up the positions constructed for us within policies. This is a system of practices (marketing one's courses, promoting one's institution) and a set of values and ethics (forcing unproductive colleagues to take early retirement so that they do not have to be counted in the departmental performativity returns). 'Discourses get things done, accomplish real tasks, gather authority' (Said 1986: 152). And we have to note the decentring of the state in this: discourses are non-reductionist. The state is here the product of discourse, a point in the diagram of power. It is a necessary but not sufficient concept in the development of an 'analytics of power' – 'The state can only operate on the basis of other, already existing power relations' (Rabinow 1986: 64), like racism and like patriarchy. I am not arguing that the state is irrelevant, or that is should not play a key role in policy analysis (see Ball 1990b). But serious attention needs to be given to the play of state power within 'disaggregated, diverse and specific (or local) sites' (Allan 1990) and to the ways in which particular fields of knowledge are sustained and challenged in these settings, around particular 'events'.

In Foucault's terms we would see policy ensembles that include, for example, the market, management, appraisal and performativity as 'regimes of truth' through which people govern themselves and others. This is based upon the production, transformation and effects of true/false distinctions (Smart 1986: 164) and the application of science and hierarchisation to 'problems' in education – like standards, discipline, the quality of teaching, efficient use of resources. These new 'sciences' of education are inhabited, disseminated and legitimated by a set of 'specific' intellectuals: the Spinks and Caldwells, Sextons, Hargreaves and Hopkins, and Fidlers and Bowles (see Chapter 6). The point of all this is that an exclusive focus upon 'secondary adjustments', particularly if this takes the form of 'naive optimism', may obscure the discursive limitations acting on and through those adjustments. We may only be able to conceive of the possibilities of response in and through the language, concepts and vocabulary which the discourse makes available to us. Thus, Offe may be right in stressing that struggle, dispute, conflict and adjustment take place over a pre-established terrain. The essence of this is that there are real struggles over the interpretation and enactment of policies. But these are set within a moving discursive frame which articulates and constrains the possibilities and probabilities of interpretation and enactment. We read and respond to policies in discursive circumstances that we cannot, or perhaps do not, think about. Also embedded in this is the intellectual work done on and in the 'politics of truth' by the advocates and technicians of policy change, and the 'will to power' and desire of those who find themselves the beneficiaries of new power relations, where power is 'exercised in the effect of one action on another action' (Hoy 1986: 135). 'Power may be understood in the first instance as the multiplicity of force relations in the sphere in which they operate and which constitute their own organization' (Foucault 1981: 92) (see Chapter 4 with regard to this). Thus, in these terms the effect of policy is primarily discursive, it changes the possibilities we have for thinking 'otherwise'; thus it limits our responses to change, and leads us to misunderstand what policy is by misunderstanding what it does. Further, policy as discourse may have the effect of redistributing 'voice', so that it does not matter what some people say or think, and only certain voices can be heard as meaningful or authoritative.

Now the danger here, of course, is that of 'naive pessimism'. As Jameson (1984: 57) puts it,

> the more powerless the reader comes to feel. In so far as the theorist wins, therefore, by constructing an increasingly closed and terrifying machine, to that very degree he [sic] loses, since the critical capacity of his work is thereby paralyzed, and the impulses of negation and revolt, not to speak of those of social transformation, are increasingly perceived as vain and trivial in the face of the model itself.

But in practice in complex modern societies we are enmeshed in a variety of discordant, incoherent and contradictory discourses, and 'subjugated knowledges' cannot be totally excluded from arenas of policy implementation (see Riseborough 1992). 'We must make allowance for the complex and unstable process whereby discourse can be both an instrument and an effect of power, but also a hindrance, a stumbling block, a point of resistance and a starting point for an opposing strategy' (Foucault 1981: 101). But we do need to recognize and analyse the existence of 'dominant' discourses, regimes of truth, erudite knowledges – like neo-liberalism and management theory – within social policy. At present I can offer no satisfactory closure on the issue of policy as discourse except, weakly perhaps, to reiterate my earlier point about needing more than one good theory to construct one half-decent explanation or account. (I tried this composite theory approach in my (1990b) study of the politics of educational reform in the UK.)

Policy effects

I want now to take up some problems remaining in the first section of the chapter in a different way. That is, by exploring how we might begin to conceptualize policy effects in a way that is neither theoretically high-handed nor trivializing. This also takes me back to my disagreement with Ozga, noted above, about the nature of localized responses to policy as being *ad hoc*, serendipitous etc. In this respect both those writers who celebrate agency and their critics misunderstand, or are at least imprecise about, what might be meant by the effects or impact of policy. I want to distinguish initially between the generalities and specifics of policy effect.

Again I want to make myself clear: the earlier discussion of policy texts is not intended to convey a conception of policy effects as typically minimal or marginal. It is not that policies have no effects, they do; it is not that those effects are not significant, they are; it is not that those effects are not patterned, they are. But to reiterate, responses (as one vehicle for effects) vary between contexts. Policies from 'above' are not the only constraints and influences upon institutional practice. One difficulty in discussing effects is that the specific and the general are often conflated. The general effects of policies become evident when specific aspects of change and specific sets of responses (within practice) are related together. A neglect of the general is most common in single-focus studies, which take one change or one policy text and attempt to determine its impact on practice. Taken in this way the specific effects of a specific policy may be limited but the general effects of ensembles of policies of different kinds may be different. I would suggest that in the UK at least (probably also in the USA, Canada, Australia and New Zealand), the cumulative and general effects of several years of multiple thrusts of educational reform on teachers' work have been profound. Here teachers' work is a general category which encompasses a variety of separate reforms related to curriculum, assessment, performativity, organization, pay and conditions (see Chapter 4). Again, though, such a generalization has to be handled carefully in at least two senses. (a) There is a danger of idealizing the past and portraying a situation in which teachers once had autonomy and now do not (again this is not a zero-sum issue). A formulation like that of Dale (1989b) of a shift from licensed to regulated autonomy is a useful tool in thinking about this. What he attempts to capture is a qualitative shift from one kind of autonomy to another; thus he has to specify the different characteristics of the two kinds. (b) The generalization will not encompass the experience of all types of teachers in all types of situation. Two examples. Teachers in the UK who find themselves in over-subscribed schools of high reputation, which can thus select students, may find their conditions of work and freedom for manoeuvre very different from teachers in under-subscribed schools of poor reputation, which must take what students they can get and will be funded at a lower level accordingly. Furthermore, the recent changes in the UK have had very different implications for classroom teachers and headteachers. The latter, in some respects, and also depending on which schools they are responsible for, find their freedom for manoeuvre and powers in relation to erstwhile colleagues enhanced rather than diminished. They are beneficiaries, at least to an extent, in the redrawing of the diagram of power (see Chapter 6). This kind of attention to policy 'effects' also highlights some other difficulties inherent in the 'policy as text' perspective. A concentration upon the interpretational responses of individual actors can lead to a neglect of the compound and structural changes effected by state policies. In particular, such a focus may lead to a neglect of the pervasive effect of institutional reconfiguration (see Chapters 4 and 5).

But there is a further important distinction to be made in regard to effects, a distinction between what might be called first order and second order effects. First order effects are changes in practice or structure (which are evident in particular sites and across the system as a whole), and second order effects are the impact of these changes on patterns of social access, opportunity and social justice. Walker (1981: 225) articulates the distinction thus:

> the essential aspect of *social* policies is their distributional implications or outcomes. Social policies may be made implicitly or explicitly, by a wide range of social institutions and groups, including the state. The task of social policy analysis is to evaluate the distributional impact of existing policies and proposals and the rationales underlying them. In such analyses attention will be focussed . . . on the behaviour of organisations, professionals and classes in order to balance descriptions of the institutional framework through which the welfare state is administered with analysis of the social production and maintenance of inequality.

One important analytical strategy which provides a mechanism for linking and tracing the discursive origins and possibilities of policy, as well as the intentions embedded in, responses to and effects of policy, is that employed by Edwards *et al.* (1989, 1992) in their APS (assisted places scheme) and CTC (city technology colleges) studies. They are what I would call policy trajectory studies. They employ a cross-sectional rather than a single level analysis by tracing policy formulation, struggle and response from within the state itself through to the various recipients of policy. Richard Bowe and I have attempted to give some conceptual structure to the trajectory method by adumbrating three contexts of policy-making (Bowe and Ball with Gold 1992): *the context of influence, the context of policy text production and the context(s) of practice.* Each context consists of a number of arenas of action – some private and some public. Each context involves struggle and compromise and ad hocery. They are loosely coupled and there is no one simple direction of flow of information between them. But in theoretical and practical terms, this model requires two further 'contexts' to make it complete. First, we must add the relationship between first order (practice) effects and second order effects; that is, *the context of outcomes.* Here analytical concern is with the issues of justice, equality and individual freedom. Policies are analysed in terms of their impact upon and interactions with existing inequalities and forms of injustice (see Chapter 7). The question of the fifth context is then begged, *the context of political strategy;* the identification of a set of political and social activities 'which might more effectively tackle inequalities' (Troyna 1993: 12). This is an essential component of what Harvey (1990) calls *critical social research* or the work of those Foucault calls 'specific intellectuals', which is produced for strategic use in particular social situations and struggles. As Sheridan (1980: 221) puts it: 'the Foucauldian genealogy is an unmasking of power for the use of those who suffer it'. This is what Foucault calls 'the real political task' in our society, 'to criticize the working of institutions which appear to be both neutral and independent, and to criticize them in such a manner that the political violence which has always exercised itself obscurely through them will be unmasked so that we can fight them' (in Rabinow 1986: 6). But Foucault's method also carries stark messages for the over-ambitious researcher/reformer; for the genealogical method, Sheridan (1980: 221) goes on to say, 'is also directed against those who would sieze power in their name'.

3

Education, Majorism and the curriculum of the dead

At last something to cheer about. The revolution in education plotted by Margaret Thatcher has gained irreversible momentum under John Major.

(*Daily Mail* 29 July 1992)

Sweeping reforms will transform the way our children are taught and the way our schools are run. The Sun welcomes them wholeheartedly. For far too long our children have been at the mercy of trendy 'experts', bolshie unions and local councils with a political axe to grind.

(*The Sun* 29 July 1992)

In this chapter I want to consider the policy dominance of 'cultural restorationism' in UK education in the 1990s. Cultural restorationists are the 'hard line, old humanists of the New Right' (Ball 1990b: 6) within the British Conservative Party, whose main policy preoccupation is with the re-valorization of traditional forms of education (Wexler and Grabiner 1986). The striking point about education policy in the UK is that since John Major replaced Margaret Thatcher as Prime Minister the cultural restorationist agenda has been in the ascendent across the whole range of school-related education policy, but particularly the curriculum, assessment, pedagogy and teacher education. In a simple sense this can be understood in terms of the capture of John Major and former Secretary of State for Education Kenneth Clarke and the incumbent John Patten by the Centre for Policy Studies (CPS), a neo-liberal/neo-conservative think-tank established by Margaret Thatcher and her New Right guru Keith Joseph after the Conservatives' election defeat in 1974. There has been an almost one-to-one relationship between CPS policy publications and Clarke's and Major's policy utterances (see below).

Clarke's successor as Secretary of State for Education, John Patten, indicated that he wished to distance himself from the CPS, and his primary policy interests (apart from his concerns about religious education and a determination that all school children be examined on their knowledge of Shakespeare) appeared not to be focused on the curriculum. However, on 14 July 1992 he appointed John Marks, a right-wing restorationist, to the National Curriculum Council (NCC). On 24 July 1992 he appointed John Marebon, CPS pamphlet writer and husband of CPS deputy director Sheila Lawlor, to the School Examinations and Assessment Council (SEAC). There was no reason to believe that John Patten's tenure would signal a real break with the restorationist agenda.

But the capture of the 'context of influence' (Bowe and Ball 1992) over policy is one thing; the translation of that influence into a credible programme of policy is another. The crucial question is how the cultural restorationist agenda has been made to look and sound credible and acceptable. I attempt to answer this question in the final section of this chapter.

While this chapter deals with the specifics of restorationist influence in UK education, the project of educational restoration is clearly evident in education systems across the English-speaking world and is also part of a wider movement of regressive traditionalism within New Right political thinking. The restorationist agenda has its basis in what Jones (1989: 32) calls 'cultural rightism'.

> It could trace its philosophy back to Hobbes and the political ideology of Burke. It emphasizes the importance of a strong state to control the evils that an unregulated society is prey to. It regards custom and tradition as vital properties of an established order. Without them, the state is weakened, and subversion can grow in strength. Thus, it regards cultural cohesion as an essential prop of state authority.

Writing of the US education system, Aronowitz and Giroux (1991) describe a similar restorationist impetus as militating around a 'cultural crisis' in education. They see the work of US restorationist writers like Bloom (1987) and Hirsch (1987) as representing

a frontal attack aimed at providing a programmatic language
with which to defend schools as cultural sites, that is as institutions responsible for reproducing the knowledge and values
necessary to advance the historical virtues of Western culture.

(Aronowitz and Giroux 1991: 25)

In their analysis Aronowitz and Giroux see textual authority and
political authority as tied tightly together within restorationist education. The aim of these 'aristocratic traditionalists', as they call them,
is 'to restore knowledge as a particular form of social authority,
pedagogy and discipline' (p. 39).

Restorationism and policy influence in the UK

There is a further complication involved in the analysis of the dominance achieved by restorationism. To appreciate fully what has
occurred we must consider what (and who) it was that the restorationists managed to replace in the 'context of influence' over policy.
Under Major and Clarke the losers in the policy making arena
were a coalition of educational 'modernizers': a loosely constituted
group made up of 'new progressive' educators, especially from the
science and mathematics education communities, and 'progressive
vocationalists' representing the educational concerns of many of the
UK's largest multinational companies (see Ball 1990b for a full discussion of these groups). In the displacement of these influences a
massive shift has taken place in the signification of education and education reform. The 'theoretical' and the 'innovative' in education have
been replaced, as the signifiers of reform, by 'tradition'. As with other
moments of reform in UK education since the Second World War,
the skill of the restorationists (with massive discursive support from
the popular media) was to be able to blame 'change' for educational
problems almost before such change has begun to have effect. The
reform process set in train by the 1988 Education Reform Act (ERA)
was wrestled away from the modernizers and reworked as a reassertion
of traditional forms of education and curriculum. In some ways this
is more than a little surprising given the strength of the industrial
lobby in UK education during the 1980s, which almost saw the
swallowing up of the Department of Education by the Department of
Employment to form a 'mega-department' of education and training (as happened in Australia in the mid-1980s). But what this

turn-around in influence points up is the more general contradictions that exist within Conservatism between the traditionalist and
modernizing tendencies. Within education this is, in crude terms, a
contradiction between the emphasis on continuity within the former
and the emphasis on planned change within the latter. Jones (1989:
82) puts it like this:

> Thus, while no opponent of selection, the modernizing tend-
> ency has no time for the grammar school tradition. Unlike the
> cultural right, it considers it to be part of the problem, not the
> solution. It is thoroughly critical of the anti-industrial values of
> a liberal education.

The sudden replacement of Thatcher with Major as UK Prime
Minister in 1990 and the cabinet re-shuffle which followed it provided the restorationists with a opportunity to respond to Major's
attempt at some kind of populist politics. His search for 'new' policies
found the right-wing think-tanks (CPS etc.) well prepared with ready-
made restorationist policies. Professor Brian Cox, one time doyen
of the traditionalist critique of educational modernization, offered
another more sinister explanation for the restorationist capture of
education policy within the Conservative Party. In a newspaper article
he suggested that:

> Since the general election a persistent rumour has been going
> round in education that the prime minister has agreed to do
> a deal with right wing Conservatives. They will go quiet in their
> opposition to Maastricht if he will allow them to take control
> of education. What truth there is in this I do not know, but it
> certainly fits the situation which has emerged in the last few
> months.
>
> (*The Guardian* 15 September 1992)

Whichever 'explanation' one accepts, the changes in policy and
policy influence since 1990 can be plotted very clearly. In the first
phases of the post-1988 reform process the 'educational establishment' was clearly 'part of the game'. Liberal professors, HMI (Her
Majesty's Inspectorate of Schools), DES officials and local educational authority (LEA) figures were all in evidence working in and
around the two newly created agencies of educational change: the
National Curriculum Council (NCC) and the Schools Examination
and Assessment Council (SEAC), the former chaired by an ex-LEA

man (Duncan Graham) and the latter by an ex-DES official (Philip Halsey). For the cultural restorationists who had argued for and supported the ERA this looked like defeat snatched from the jaws of victory. Those people whose views and influence they had sought to supplant by the strictures and requirements of the ERA were the very people given the task of filling in and implementing the reform agenda.

> The main source of trouble has been successive Ministers allow-ing the crucial committees, commissions and working parties charged with the detailed implementation of the Act to be dominated by the same sort of people, and sometimes the very same people, as have been responsible for reducing our main-tained school system to the catastrophic condition which that 1988 Act was supposed to remedy. These 'progressive egalitar-ians' remain more or less openly resolved to frustrate the re-forming purposes of the 1988 Act. It is significant that among the original appointees to the National Curriculum Council and the Schools Examination and Assessment Council there was not even one person who had been prominent among the longtime critics calling for radical reform of the previous estab-lishment [in other words, not one of 'us'].
>
> (Flew 1991: 43)

One indication of the effect of this kind of critique on Major and Clarke came in July 1991 when Philip Halsey, Chairman and Chief Executive of SEAC, and Duncan Graham, Chairman of the NCC, were both removed from their posts, the latter to be replaced by Lord Griffiths of Fforestfach, formerly Head of Mrs Thatcher's advi-sory team at No. 10 Downing Street. When appointed to the NCC, Lord Griffiths, a former professor of economics at City University, was Chairman of the Centre for Policy Studies; absolutely 'one of us'. David Pascall, another former advisor to Margaret Thatcher, became Chairman of the NCC. By mid-1992 it could be said that the cul-tural restorationists of the Conservative New Right, members of the CPS in particular, were well entrenched as the 'new' 'educational establishment'.[1]

In effect, the implementation of the ERA has become the terrain for policy in-fighting over the determination of the three basic mes-sage systems of schooling (Bernstein 1971): curriculum, assessment and, more recently, pedagogy. Representing this struggle for control of the definition of 'what it means to be educated' are two contrasting images of the school: the cultural restorationist image of the Victorian schoolroom and the modernizers' image of the flexible, post-Fordist school. But before I go on to unpack these images further I want to spend some time illustrating the issues at stake in each of the three areas of struggle.

The curriculum

The most visible aspect of the Conservative government's educational reforms is the development and installation of the National Curriculum. Not since the nineteenth-century Revised Codes has a UK government attempted to assert direct control over the school curriculum; although the examination system and university entrance requirements have always served as significant forms of surrogate control. But during the 1970s and 1980s it became the received wisdom within the Conservative Party that the school curriculum was out of control; that 'real' knowledge was being replaced, especially in comprehensive secondary and progressive primary schools, by an 'ideological curriculum'. Mrs Thatcher took up this concern in her speech to the 1987 Party Conference.

> Too often our children don't get the education they need – the education they deserve. And in the inner cities – where youngsters must have a decent education if they are to have a better future – that opportunity is all too often snatched from them by hard-left educational authorities and extremist teachers. Children who need to be able to count and multiply are learning anti-racist mathematics – whatever that may be. Children who need to be able to express themselves in clear English are being taught political slogans. Children who need to be taught to respect traditional moral values are being taught that they have an inalienable right to be gay.

The National Curriculum, then, is intended to put 'real' knowledge back into school and to discipline teachers. But the 'will to truth' underlying the reform has not been easy to realize, despite the enormous range of new powers accruing to the Secretary of State for Education from the 1988 ERA. Even a very careful selection of members of the Subject Working Groups (one for each of the ten National Curriculum subjects) did not prevent the occurrence of several very public disagreements over the contents and orientation of the Working Group Reports. On a number of occasions the process of curriculum specification was reduced to the assertion of a set of personal prejudices held by the incumbent Secretary of State (urged on by cultural restorationist supporters) over and against the best judgement of Working Group members and subject practitioners (see Ball 1990b: 198–204, on the Mathematics Working Party). The political agenda for the National Curriculum was never very far from the surface in these encounters. I want to present three brief examples of these struggles, each of which highlights aspects of cultural restorationism; they relate to music, geography and history.

Music

Music has always been a subject backwater in the school curriculum, a matter of little interest to most students and hardly a focus of political controversy. The cultural restorationist response to the Music Working Party report and the Secretary of State's subsequent intervention changed all that. The reaction to the Report was orchestrated by two newspaper articles, both written by cultural restorationist philosophers, organic intellectuals of the New Right, Anthony O'Hear (1991b) and Roger Scruton (1991). The Report was described as 'a betrayal of the nation's children' and of 'the classical tradition . . . the highest achievement of European culture'. The focus of the philosophers' ire was the proposal that one of three main Attainment Targets for music should be *performance*. What the writers of the Report had dared to do was to represent school music as having elements of both knowledge and participation; that is, to attempt to write into the National Curriculum the idea (already a well accepted approach in school classrooms) that learning music could involve making music as well as learning *about* music. By devoting one Attainment Target to the musical experience of the student, their musical efforts were, in the eyes of the critics, being equated somehow with the products of the European canon. The restorationist response reduced a set of complex issues to a matter of Beethoven (always Beethoven) versus steel bands.

Two key aspects of the restorationist project are touched upon here: the distrust of experience and relevance, and the Eurocentric, cultural racism that informs their aesthetic judgements. The former is illustrated in a passage from Scruton's article, which suggests an extraordinary personal alienation: 'But when I was 15, playing bass guitar and piano with my mates, I already knew that what I did could be of no lasting value to me. This knowledge came to me because I had been taught to value *music*.' The point here is that *music* is defined solely in terms of product, in terms of what others, listed in the canon, do. For the restorationists music is not a putting together of sounds to create effect or a shared activity, it is not a matter of creativity but rather a lonely appreciation, a fossilized tradition, a mental abstraction divorced from the here and now and from the possibility of engagement. Education and learning here are founded upon alienation, a negation of self; knowledge is valued precisely for its irrelevance, esotericism, detachment, elitism and intrinsic difficulty; learning is an act of abasement, of passivity, of deference. The learner comes to knowledge naive and innocent and leaves that which is learned untouched and unchanged. This is the curriculum as museum. Significantly, Scruton's approved repertoire fails to name a single living composer. Daringly, O'Hear includes Duke Ellington in his list, although this would presumably have met with the approval of jazz fan Kenneth Clarke.

The Secretary of State's personal response to the Working Party Report and the subsequent NCC Consultation Report left little doubt as to whose views counted when the National Curriculum was at stake. An editorial in the practitioners' journal *Music Teacher* (February 1992: 5) reported:

> The publication of the NCC Consultation Report on Music has caused fury among music teachers and educationalists ... [it] alters its balance away from performing and in favour of factual knowledge and suggests that western classical music be given prominence over music of other cultures ... The NCC has merely implemented the Education Secretary's desire for simplification, factual learning and an emphasis on the western classical heritage ... The Report acknowledges that not only is it rejecting the main thrust of the Working Group's report, it is also discounting the support it received ... 80% of respondents agreed with the Attainment Targets proposed.

The NCC Consultation Report on Music had concluded that 'Council does not consider that the Working Group's proposals for three

Attainment targets places sufficient emphasis on the History of Music, on diverse musical heritage and on the appreciation of a variety of other musical traditions.'

In the case of music the cultural restorationists saw the subject as having been captured by progressive educators. In the case of geography, progressive educators (and many other practitioners) saw the initial working party report as having been captured by or strongly influenced by the cultural restorationist agenda.

Geography

The controversies over the Geography Working Group Report cover similar ground, particularly the Secretary of State's concern for more emphasis on factual learning. But in this case the initial draft of the Report was the object of practitioner's concerns. Many geographers saw themselves and their subject being deskilled and depoliticized by a return to a simplified regional geography approach. School geography was to be fragmented, as they saw it, with the effect that spatial, economic, political and ecological aspects of the subject would be divorced from one another (Huckle and Machon 1990). Commentators discerned a strong Conservative political agenda embedded in the Report.

> Why should California feature so strongly, without any require-
> ment to undertake a serious study of China? The naming of the
> Falkland Islands could be seen as one instance of highlighting
> detail for its own sake and the re-establishment of Capes and
> Bays which had taken 50 years of hard campaigning to dis-
> establish in the late sixties; alternatively its inclusion might be
> seen as a political statement which reifies our Imperial Tradi-
> tion, which is symbolically out of keeping with our economic
> future within a European Community. Is Colonel Blimp to haunt
> us forever either through the specification of factual knowl-
> edge as an end in itself, or of particular places which are tomb-
> stones of the past?
>
> (Hall 1990: 314)

What is striking again in these proposals is the backward lookingness of the conception of subject knowledge. The Report appears to aim at a repositioning of the UK in some mythical golden age of empire.

Geography is tied into an unstated politics of space. At times the proposals seem to have more to do with Margaret Thatcher's policies on Europe than good educational practice. The emphasis is upon the subordination of the learner to place and space rather than on analytical control. Distance is a fact here rather than a stance. The learner is lost in untheorized space and is left only with a list of memorized capitals. Despite some recovery of lost ground in the final report, the thrust and intonation of school geography have been reoriented. With its undertones of assimilation, nationalism and consensus around the regressive re-establishment of fictional past glories, restorationist National Curriculum geography isolates students in time and space, cutting them off from the realities of a single European market, global economic dependencies and inequalities, and ecological crisis.

History

Similar comments can be addressed to history, although the emotive background to the History Report is stronger. In the 1988 Conservative Party Conference, the then Secretary of State, Kenneth Baker, announced his determination to ensure that in future all children would learn the key events in British history, including 'the spread of Britain's influence for good throughout the world', and added that 'we should not be ashamed of our history, our pride in our past gives us our confidence to stand tall in the world today'. Again the restorationist crusade against the curriculum reforms of the 1960s and 1970s, in this case 'new history', provided a driving force of assertion and critique (Beattie 1987; Kedourie 1988; Deucher 1989) to underpin National Curriculum History. Thus, in a CPS publication *On the Evils and Errors of New History*, Kedourie (1988: 5–6) explains:

> The purpose of this paper is to disclose to the general reader some of the ways in which, under the guise of history, which is one of the foundation subjects of the proposed national curriculum, secondary schoolchildren are being introduced to a subject very different to anything which their parents are likely to have been taught; which indeed resembles traditional history not at all. The situation is serious; many children are now leaving school with no historical knowledge at all. History itself is to be

understood in terms of concepts such as cause and effect, change
and development, progress and continuity. Students are to feel
that they can take part in history and that they have an active
part to play. Their comprehension of the subject is to be fostered through empathy.

The coincidence of pedagogical and political critique here hardly
needs comment. The shock and horror which run through all the
restorationist criticisms of 'new history' are a reaction against the
possibility that students could or should be encouraged to see their
lives and experiences as linked to, part of, history, or to see themselves as makers of history. Restorationist history is a set of facts
about the past made up of key events and famous people; it has
its own passive momentum. There is no room for theory or analysis.
As above, attempts to see beyond events to their causes or to link
events together by explanations are regarded with profound suspicion.
History is there to be learned, known about. Such a conception does
profound political and pedagogical work. It 'effectively abolishes any
practical sense of the future and of the collective project, thereby
abandoning the thinking of future change to fantasies of sheer ca-
tastrophe and inexplicable cataclysm' (Jameson 1984: 65). Restorationist history is 'the reconstruction of the past for its own sake',
not a 'prelude to current affairs' (Beattie 1987: 4). It is a value-free
history that divorces fact from interpretation and interpretation from
interest. We are left with the 'impersonal authority of tradition' (Jones
1989). It is in these terms that we can interpret the Secretary of
State's response to the History Working Group's Interim Report. He
(John MacGregor on this occasion) asserted that:

1 Chronology deserves greater emphasis.
2 The proportion of British history should be increased.
3 Knowledge should be included as a separate Attainment Target.

Mrs Thatcher (then still Prime Minister) also made her opposition
to the Interim Report known at this time, and the restorationist
changes to the Final Report were attributed in some quarters to her
intervention. Thus the newspaper headlines ran: 'Thatcher's conquest
on history in schools' (*Daily Express* 4 April 1990) and 'Thatcher has
her way over school history' (*Independent on Sunday* 1 April 1990).
    The links between past and present in restorationist history are

very different from those of 'new history'. The 'past glories' approach serves the ideology of empire and nationalism. The blood, struggle, pain and mess of history is reworked into a litany of glories and victories, a retrospective and sentimental adjustment of the actual. This is part of what Foucault calls 'the struggle over popular memory'. In restorationist history Britain is to be at the centre of history, a benign and progressive influence upon the world, bearer of justice and civilization. The focus, taken up in the National Curriculum documentation, is upon political, constitutional and military history rather than social or cultural. School history is envisioned as a poetics of power played out as a soap opera of kings, queens and courtiers, as spectacle and personality. Emotion, identification, re-morse and empathy are to be excised and instead we have history as a reconstitutive moral force and as a celebration of oppression and violence (articulated via the recurring imperial referent).

> The phenomenon of National Curriculum history can be seen clearly as an attempt by those with the power to do it (a demo-cratically elected government) to try and construct what seems to it to be an appropriate past. Here a government, a working group, SEAC and the NCC, acting as our historians, have been busy designing the past so that it might act as the vehicle for the transmission of culture.
>
> (Jenkins and Brickley 1990: 11)

Across these three subjects the assertion of the restorationist cur-riculum has a striking uniformity in both form and content. In each case, the starting point is the deconstruction of the comprehensive, modernist curriculum and then its replacement with a political but depoliticized, authoritative curriculum of tradition. This employs what I have called elsewhere 'the discourse of derision' (Ball 1990b). Simple polarities are deployed within this discourse, based upon the certain-ties of 'good' and 'evil', the sacred and profane, and sanity and lunacy. Foucault's (1971: 11) second principle of exclusion – divi-sion and rejection – is very much in evidence here. The language, style and tone of moral outrage leave no grounds for professional judgement in these areas. There is no doubt, no compromise, no relativism. *This is curricular fundamentalism.* Moral positions are clear, absolute and general. The modernist project of comprehensive education is damned and rejected root and branch. In each case, the attempt to recognize the pluralism and multiculturalism of late twentieth-century Britain is derided and replaced by a regressive 'little Englandism'. 'We are facing an enormous challenge, possibly the biggest in our whole history. Our civilization is threatened not only by cultures with different attitudes and values, but by destructive tendencies within ourselves' (Deucher 1989: 1). In each case, the links between pedagogy and knowledge, experience and understanding are severed and replaced by authoritative texts and authoritative teaching. The student is to learn from history and about music and geography but is separate from them. The possibilities of analytical or political consciousness or of participation in 'culture' are excluded. Not surprisingly, this curriculum of transmission is neatly packaged with equally uncompromising and traditionalist visions of assessment and pedagogy. The terrain of dispute over pedagogy and assessment is, not surprisingly, established across the contending versions of the nature of knowledge adumbrated above. It is to these I now turn, although again briefly.

Assessment

Here the issue at stake is superficially very simple: how best to assess the student. But as ever this simplicity masks a set of difficult philosophical and psychological debates (see Troman 1989). I have the space here only to scratch the surface. The battlelines between the 'old' educational establishment – in favour of diagnostic, problem solving, open-ended, process-oriented, teacher assessments – and the cultural restorationists – in favour of publishable, measurement-based, competitive, pencil and paper, externally set tests and examinations – are well established. The original basis for National Curriculum assessment (the TGAT Report, DES 1988a) was fairly firmly on the former model. Subsequent changes recommended by SEAC or made unilaterally by Secretaries of State signal a decisive move towards the latter. Secretary of State Clarke summed up the restorationist position in his Westminster Lecture of 1991 (Clarke 1991b):

> The British pedagogue's hostility to written examinations of any kind can be taken to ludicrous extremes. The British left believe that pencil and paper examinations impose stress on pupils and demotivate them. [Note the casual juxtapositioning

of 'pedagogues' and 'the left'.] We have tolerated for 20 years an arrangement whereby there is no national testing or examination of any kind for most pupils until they face GCSE at the age of 16 . . . This remarkable national obsession lies behind the more vehement opposition to the recent introduction of seven year old testing. They were made a little too complicated [the TGAT model] and we have said we will simplify them . . . The complications themselves were largely designed in the first place in an attempt to pacify opponents who feared above all else 'paper and pencil tests' . . . This opposition to testing and examinations is largely based on a folk memory in the left about the old debate on the 11-plus and grammar schools.

Here, then, *complex* assessment is seen as designed to obscure. *Simple* tests are revealing. Complexity is 'soft', misleading, producer-based. Simplicity is 'hard', clear, unequivocal and commonsensical. For the restorationists testing is a way of differentiating between students and identifying 'poor' schools; for the neo-liberal wing of the New Right test results also provide the information system which they believe will drive the market in education. In part also, the restorationist attacks upon coursework and teacher assessments rest on a fundamental distrust of the teacher. '"Pupil profiles" constructed by the pupils' own teachers are not to be relied on save in so far as they can be and are cross-checked against the findings of independently assessed public examinations' (Flew 1991: 29). Assessments are seen to have little or no pedagogic value; rather they must serve as performance indicators of teacher effectivity. Thus, coursework assessment is taken as 'a call to abandon a fundamental principle of natural justice – that no one should be judge of their own cause' (Flew 1991: 29). This is further indication of the restorationists' extraordinary philosophy and social psychology of distrust, rooted in a belief in the worst in all of us, in a norm of rational self-interest, which gives rise to the need for discipline and incentives as the only possible bases for social order and social motivation.

Pedagogy

The previous Secretary of State Kenneth Clarke reserved his particular views and concerns about teaching and learning for an assault

upon the progressive movement in primary education. In a lecture
to the Tory Reform Group (Clarke 1991b), drawing heavily upon a
CPS pamphlet (O'Hear 1990b), Clarke mounted a critique of 'progressive' and 'child-centred' education and the 'trendy progressive
views of "expert" educationalists'. In particular, in an extraordinary
series of misreadings, logical leaps and non sequiturs, he argued that
educational theory, and especially the theories of Rousseau and
Dewey, had led to a neglect of knowledge in primary schools and a
sentimental idealization of the child.

> Rousseau is the root of much of the position of the left on this
> as on so many other things. Rousseau's philosophy has been
> developed by John Dewey to form a basis for an ideology of
> modern education and one which has taken root in some of
> our schools, colleges and departments of education. His ideas
> are symptomatic of a whole philosophy of life which tends to
> be dismissive of what has been learned in the past. Dewey's
> hostility to traditional learning and to tradition in general stem
> from his belief that the child is or should be primarily con-
> cerned with working out his own answers to his own problems.
> Hence the so-called child-centred approach to teaching that
> he advocates. The child will be taught to discount custom and
> tradition. Dewey and his followers overlook the way in which
> any field of human activity (including the scientific inciden-
> tally) will contain a mass of customary and traditional know-
> ledge and skills.
>
> (Clarke 1991b: 5)

It is questionable whether this is a recognizable account of Deweyan
thought, but within this discourse accuracy is irrelevant. It is *effect* that
counts – the destabilization of commitment and of respect. What is
central here again is the deification of tradition and of the past and
a trenchant opposition to any recognition of the child as active within
the learning process. This discursive intervention into primary school
teaching methods was followed up in December 1991 by the an-
nouncement by the Secretary of State of a 'debate among primary
teachers about how children can most effectively be taught' (letter
11 December 1991) (learning is of little consequence in all this). His
earlier statement on 'primary education' explained:

> Let me be quite clear, however, that questions about how to
> teach are not for the Government to determine. I have no

intention to seek to extend my powers in that direction. My
purpose is to initiate a discussion, not to impose solutions . . .
I am asking every primary head teacher and every primary
classroom teacher to join in the radical rethinking now needed
as to how best to teach children in our schools.

(Clarke 1991a: 2)

What is unclear in the statement is how the debate should progress.
How would teachers make their views known? How would the outcomes be decided? Why should the debate be constrained to a 'radical rethinking'? No recourse to tradition and custom for teachers!
The point is, of course, that this is no 'real' debate, it is a language
game, it is the erection of a discursive platform from which the
Secretary of State can speak about things he acknowledges as being
beyond the scope of his powers. The debate is no event, there are
no moments for speaking, there is no collection of views or evidence (apart from those orchestrated by the Secretary of State). It
all depends upon the ability to make oneself heard. Thus, the anti-
educationalist media joined in with gusto. *The Evening Standard* (9
December 1991: 9) announced, under the headline 'The woman
behind 25 lost years of children's education' (referring to Lady
Plowden), that

Last week Her Majesty's Inspectors of Education declared that
British primary school teachers could learn much from their
French counterparts. Blackboards, desks, formal disciplined
teaching and the return of streaming could soon become per-
manent features of our classrooms, concludes the report.

The villain of the piece, according to *Standard* reporter Melanie
McDonagh, is Lady Plowden (Chairperson of the 1967 pro-progressive Plowden Report). The Secretary of State summed up the HMI
report, referred to in the *Standard* article:

HMI are publishing this week a report on primary education in
France. Teachers worked through a highly centralised National
Curriculum, with classes of similar size to those in England.
Whole class and didactic teaching was used extensively. HMI
found that such teaching was thoroughly planned, effectively
implemented and challenging, and that children progressed
well. Pupils concentrated on the task set and responded positively to demanding work.

(Clarke 1991a: 5)

In his statement Secretary Clarke announced that 'To help focus the debate and inform policy on the training of primary teachers, I have commissioned a report from Professor Robin Alexander, Chief Inspector Jim Rose of HMI and Christopher Woodhead, Chief Executive of the National Curriculum Council, on primary teaching methods and classroom organisation.' In effect, the debate was opened, judged and closed in the same document. Progressive child-centred methods and the Plowden Report were subjected to a public deconstruction, progressive teachers were disciplined and the groundwork was laid for a thoroughgoing reintroduction of traditional teaching methods. Indeed (except for discursive effect) there was no need for debate. It follows clearly from the fundamentalist approach to knowledge that learning is ritual, an initiation into heritage, a means of preserving and reproducing the canon.

Common sense and Victorianism

Running through all of this are a set of key themes and images. One of the themes, which is a key feature of Majorism more generally, is an *anti-intellectualism*; that is, a distrust of theory and research and over and against these the assertion of common sense, epitomized by John Major's 'university of the streets'. This is a natural extension of the Thatcherite celebration of the streetwise, real-world entrepreneur and concomitant denigration of the theory-driven, red-tape, public servant. Pecuniary self-interest is preferred to bureaucratic self-interest. The discursive privileging of common sense also underwrites the unimpeachability of the canon. The *natural* superiority and status of the canon are part of common sense, and the gate-keepers and arbiters thus remain invisible. To question the canon is to go against common sense, is irrational, is destructive and mad.

A second theme is *nostalgia*, an educational Victorianism which represents education, to parents in particular, in terms of familiar images of 'traditional' pedagogic forms. This is a form of cultural populism organized around notions of discipline, authority and learning. The Victorian schoolroom and the grammar school are the lost objects of desire, standing for a time when education was simple, when learning meant doing and knowing what you were told by your teacher. Kenneth Clarke's classroom has desks in rows, the children silent, the teacher 'at the front', chalk in hand, dispensing knowledge. This powerful image of 'the teacher' and of 'teaching' makes perfect sense to parents in ways that new teaching methods and new teacher–student relationships do not. Many recognize in this fragments, images and laments of their own schooling. Of course, this is not what traditional classrooms were actually like most of the time for most people. This is historicism as policy: 'namely the random cannibalisation of all the styles of the past, the play of random stylistic allusion, and in general what Henri Lefebvre has called the increasing primacy of the "neo"' (Jameson 1984: 65–6).

Thus, 'traditional education' (and traditional values) is here a pastiche, a policy simulacrum – the identical copy for which no original has ever existed. UK education policy is now set within what Jameson (1984: 66) calls 'the nostalgia mode': 'the desperate attempt to appropriate a missing past', to return education to a state of naivety and innocence before special learning needs, worksheets, problem-solving, investigations, reading readiness and constructivism. Here learning is based on teaching and intelligence; teaching is about fixed and agreed knowledges (and knowledge is also constituted by the past) and intelligence is measured by tests. Not surprisingly, this simulacrum coincides perfectly with the broader agenda of restorationism and the neo-conservative project to re-establish *order and place*. This is an education of deference, to the teacher, to the past, to the nation, and to your 'elders and betters' – the traditional values of Victorian middle-class childhood. Hierarchy and differentiation are naturalized within this discourse of 'authority'. This is an attempt to remove education from its contemporary context; to create instead a regressive fantasy education, the school as historical theme park, where past styles are the 'referents' for the methods of the new teacher.

Underpinning conduct in the restorationist classroom are the twin virtues of the Majorite classless society: individualism (of a kind) and competition. These are set over and against the collective modernism of the comprehensive school. The classroom is a microcosm of the whole society: 'conservatives can happily value both the historic traditions of this country and the values of freedom and the free market' (Willetts 1992: 108). The ontology of restorationism is opposed to any conception of human nature as social (except in the narrow senses of family and nation) and conceives instead of private, self-sufficient competing individuals; this is founded on the politics and economics of Adam Smith and Fredrich Hayek. The belief in the Victorian *laissez-faire* economy (and its peculiar mercantile naturalism, realized in tradition and history, and notions of market-driven economic Darwinism) is paralleled in the idea of intellectual natural selection in the classroom. Teaching is not so much a pedagogic intervention as the most effective method for identifying and realizing inevitable intelligence-based differences between students.

And knowledge in the traditional schoolroom is realized via the traditional curriculum, the preservation and transmission of the 'best of all that has been said and written'; itself a pastiche, an edited, stereotypical, unreal, schoolbook past. It is a curriculum which eschews relevance and the present, concentrating on 'the heritage' and 'the canon', based on 'temporal disengagement'; a curriculum suspicious of the popular and the immediate, made up of echoes of past voices, the voices of a cultural and political elite; a curriculum which ignores the pasts of women and the working class and the colonized – *a curriculum of the dead*. Reverence and detachment are the acceptable educational stances within this pantheon approach to knowledge; rather different from any sense of 'critical distance'. This 'effectively abolishes any practical sense of the future and the collective project' (Jameson 1984: 85). The canon is unchallengeable. The selections are done elsewhere, at other times, they are 'handed down' by the unassailable 'judgement of generations'. The Plowdonian child as active learner is replaced by the silent reader and patient listener. The schoolroom is a place of hush and the pupil is rendered incapable of fashioning representations of her own current experience. 'However large the girocheque may be, if the person receiving it has had such a bad education that they do not know who Winston Churchill was, and have never come into contact with the writing of Charles Dickens, then they are indeed at risk of being disinherited from their own community' (Willetts 1992: 118). Here community is a community of the past, a deferential heritage, cultural rallying points for forging national identity, consensus and political affiliation. Culture (with a big 'C') replaces politics (and economics) as the basis for making sense of experience. Experience is made possible through a discourse of 'edited highlights' from the glossy mirage of historicism.

The success of restorationism lies in the familiarity of its referents. It replaces the uncertainties of change with cosy, sepia images of family, nation and school which are tied into an ensemble of nostalgia. The order and common sense virtues of the Victorian schoolroom provide a powerful counterpoint to the immense glass and plastic anonymity of the modernist comprehensive school. The populist politics of Majorism, which replaces equality with 'classlessness', renaturalizes an education system which achieves commonality by division and legitimates difference by the ideology of choice. In the restorationists' education system value and worth are generated not by the complexities of teaching and learning but by the iconography of the school uniform, the examination hall and the authoritarian teacher. Signifier and signified are rent asunder. The past, present and future of schooling coalesce so that change and progress are achieved by a return to a fantasy past; individual freedom is partnered by patriarchal sternness; economic regeneration is to be based on forms of teaching and learning quite unrelated to the flexible specialization required by post-Fordist production techniques. Thus, restorationist philosopher O'Hear is dubious even of the Conservative government's invention of city technology colleges, and warns that the products of these schools may become the Bob Cratchits of the future, 'tied to their computer screens without even the Victorian clerk's pride in his handwriting' (O'Hear cited in Regan 1990; see also O'Hear 1988).

Note

1 In 1993 the NCC and SEAC were abolished and replaced by the School Curriculum and Assessment Authority (SCAA); Griffiths and Pascall were replaced by Sir Ron Dearing. Dearing certainly cannot be identified with Thatcherism or New Rightism.

4

Education policy, power relations and teachers' work

In this chapter I examine the increasingly over-determined and over-regulated situation of schoolteachers' work and the matrix of power relations in which they are enmeshed. Specifically, I will be concerned with the three main forms of control which are being used in the UK in an attempt to capture, specify and delineate 'teaching': the curriculum, the market and management. All of this seems to indicate a radical attempt to reconstruct and redefine the meaning and purpose of teaching, both as vocational practice and as mental labour. I shall spend most time on the third form – management – but to establish my argument I must also give some indication of the changing power relations of the curriculum (see also Chapter 3) and the market. In the development of this analysis I intend to draw in part on the work of Michel Foucault. At times I will employ his extravagant language and I use Foucault's dystopia of 'hierarchical observation' as a heuristic device. I do this to achieve some analytic distance from and leverage upon power relations in current educational policies and in order to translate a debate which is often conducted in a neutral technical language into, in his terms, an 'analytics of power'. I will illustrate some of the points I make with some extracts from research data. The analysis as a whole is summarized in Figure 4.1.

The curriculum and the classroom

In simple terms, here I refer to the imposition of a national curriculum and national testing, and direct and indirect interventions into

Figure 4.1

	Curriculum	*The market*	*Management*
Forms of control	commonality	variety	consensus?
	prescription	mechanism	self-regulation
	intervention	responsivity	flexibility
System steering	*ex post* processual and *ex ante*	reputation *ex ante*	*ex post*/feedback
Teacher as	deliverer	commodity-producer	resource
	tester	performer	accountable
	technician	entrepreneur?	cost
Changes in	the balance between local and central curriculum	the values and the professional culture of the institution	the relationship of the managers and the managed

pedagogical decision making. The three basic message systems of schooling are thus subject to change, and changes in any one system interrelate with and affect the others. In general terms there is an increase in the technical elements of teachers' work and a reduction in the professional. Significant parts of teachers' practice are now codified in terms of Attainment Targets and Programmes of Study, and measured in terms of Standard Attainment Tasks. The spaces for professional autonomy and judgement are (further) reduced (see Dale 1989b: Chapter 8). A standardization and normalization of classroom practice is being attempted. The curriculum provides for standardization and testing for normalization – the establishment of measurements, hierarchy and regulation around the idea of a distributionary statistical norm within a given population. This begins with the testing of students, but raises the possibility of monitoring

the performance of teachers and schools and making comparisons between them. There is also the possibility of linking these
comparisons to appraisal and to performance-related pay awards.
Performance-related pay schemes are already being piloted in UK
schools. These developments also relate to what Lyotard (1984) calls
the 'legitimation of education through performativity'. I shall return
to this later. Furthermore, significant changes in teachers' classroom
practice can now be achieved by decisions taken 'at a distance' about
assessment regimes or curriculum organization. Thus, the reduction
of coursework elements in GCSE assessment has profound implications for classroom work. And the introduction of separate programmes of study in National Curriculum subjects (most recently
English) can 'dictate' the form of student grouping in the school.
The possibility of the publication and comparison of test scores may
also play a part in teachers' decision making about how much time
to devote to whole-class and individual work, or their distribution of
attention between different students in the classroom. In all this
there is an increasing concern about the quality, character and content of teachers' labour and increasingly direct attempts made by the
state to shape the character and content of classroom practice.

Another form of intervention into pedagogy (see Chapter 3) is
currently centred upon primary schooling and the campaign among
conservative cultural restorationists to re-establish streaming and class
teaching. Concomitantly, methods associated with progressivism are
under attack (Alexander *et al.* 1992). What is important here is not
so much what is being asserted in the 'debate' over methods as the
'effect' of these assertions in decentring the teacher. What is achieved
is a redistribution of significant voices. As always, it is a matter not
just of what is said but of who is entitled to speak. The teacher is
increasingly an absent presence in the discourses of education policy,
an object rather than a subject of discourse. I shall explore this point
more fully later.

We're into a situation now where I think we are definitely not
in control, I don't feel in control. I may feel consulted, but the
consultations are more or less about what has been discussed
and decided . . . even the style of heads of departments is becoming like that too, they're finding their room for manoeuvre
is not that great either. So I'm not blaming them so much,
they're being told to implement things, therefore they're coming

over as being quite, not perhaps dictatorial, that's too harsh a
phrase, but perhaps as being determinedly persuasive, 'that's
what's going to happen'. And no doubt they're looking over
their shoulder, because they're being told, 'look, you are the
one that's accountable, so get these things done'. And that's it,
the directive is taking shape.

(Experienced teacher, Flightpath Comprehensive)

One of the worst things about the changes here is that we are
not allowed to discuss them properly at staff meetings. If we
raise an intelligent question, we are accused of being negative.
Critical thinking, logical reasoning, all outlawed. You have to
decode everything these days. When they say, 'we had a productive meeting', they mean no real discussion took place.
Everyone nodded approval. Another success for the mindless
public relations world we are creating.

(Mr Osborne, Brian Baru School, quoted in
Mac an Ghaill 1991: p 307)

The market

The second element in the changing matrix of power within which
schools are set also has far-reaching implications for the redefinition
of teachers' work. The introduction of market forces into the relations between schools means that teachers are now working within a
new value context, in which image and impression management are
becoming as important as the educational process (see Chapter 8).
Furthermore, in some schools the locus of control is shifting from
the producer (teachers) to the consumer (parents) via open enrolments, parental choice and per capita funding (see Chapters 6 and
7). The market is a disciplinary system and within it education is
reconstructed as a consumption good. Children and their 'perform-
ances' are traded and exchanged as commodities. In relations between schools, the key element of the market is competition. 'The
competitive process provides incentives and so evokes effort . . . The
essence of the whole process is choice by the consumer; emulation,
rivalry and substitution by the producer' (Reekie 1984: 37). Teachers' work is thus increasingly viewed and evaluated solely in terms of
output measures (test scores and examination performance) set
against cost (subject time, class size, resource requirements).

The processes of competition in education are driven by price and by supply and demand, much the same as in other markets, except that in contrast to most commodity markets prices are fixed in relation to LEA budgets and a DfE approved formula. The onus is upon schools to attract clients and maximize income. Marketing and income generation are presently major priorities in the planning and decision making activities of senior managers in many schools (Bowe and Ball with Gold 1992). In some schools the discourses of financial planning and economic rationalism now operate in an antagonistic relation to the discourses of teaching and learning and pupil welfare.

> You are caught, and this is where LMS really raises its ugly head, in terms of true educational things. Each child has a price tag on it, and the sixth formers have the highest price tag – so, in pure financial terms, one is obviously trying to raise the most money you can. But the Flightpath staff have always been conscious of our intake being skewed towards the less able child, and through the years we've had one of the best supportive education departments in the LEA . . . But, of course, less able children tend not to stay on into the sixth form, unless we feel they really will benefit from it . . . So you have this conflict of trying to ensure that you've got a bit of a sixth form and trying to ensure that you really are doing the best for the individual child.
>
> (Senior Teacher, Flightpath Comprehensive)

The relationship of schools to 'consumers', the priorities of school organization and the ethics of impression management are all affected by the market context. The deputy head quoted below is talking about the school open evening and the headteacher's speech to parents.

> We sat down beforehand in the Senior Management Team and said, 'What do we want the Head to say?' And, basically, it was, appear traditional, conservative with a small 'c' and emphasize traditional things like hard work, discipline. Emphasize the fact that the authority don't particularly like it that we exclude quite significant numbers of pupils, more than they would like us to exclude. Particularly for fighting and particularly for bullying. Emphasize the fact that our examination results, in terms of number of GCSEs, have improved by 25 per cent over the last three years, which is not too bad. And keep it short, sharp and

keep it to those areas . . . And we are a caring institution. We have a sophisticated pastoral system, it's the backbone of the school and that was emphasized. And people, round and about, have got the impression that the pastoral system is very good. It's got a very good special needs department. Now that itself might cause problems, because if you're known to be the school to deal effectively with SEN kids you will get a higher proportion of those kids, which has resource implications and implications for the image of the institution and what the institution turns out and you may well be less comprehensive than you would want to be. So she didn't over-emphasize it. And talked about pastoral in a way that means more than looking after the welfare of children and that an integral part of it is what they achieve in terms of examination results.

(Deputy head, Trumpton School)

Here, impression management and responsiveness to the consumer are used to reorientate the values of the institution and subvert and reorder the priorities and purposes through which it presents itself (see Chapter 8). In crude terms, the important thing is to reflect back to parents their prejudices, setting aside experience and judgement. Traditionalism and academicism are accented; expertise in special needs provision is underplayed, for fear of giving the 'wrong' impression.

Management

The examples quoted above already begin to point up the intimate relationship between the control exercised over teachers by parental choice and competition and the role of management. Management and the market are clearly closely intertwined in UK government thinking. As DES Circular 7/88 indicates,

Local management is concerned with far more than budgeting and accounting procedures. Effective schemes of local management will enable governing bodies and headteachers to plan their use of resources – including their most valuable resource, their staff – to maximum effect in accordance with their own need and priorities, and to make schools more responsive to their clients – parents, pupils, the local community and employers.

(DES 1988b: 3)

Further, the point about both management and the market is that they are 'no hands' forms of control as far as the relationship between education and the state is concerned. They provide, in Kickert's (1991: 21) terms, 'steering at a distance' – a new paradigm of public governance. Steering at a distance is an alternative to coercive/prescriptive control. Constraints are replaced by incentives. Prescription is replaced by *ex post* accountability based upon quality or outcome assessments. Coercion is replaced by self-steering – the appearance of autonomy. Opposition or resistance are side-stepped, displaced.

> The refined subtle character of behavioural stimuli makes resistance difficult. The repressive tolerance of such a way of steering might cause a large latent aggression against that steering. Organisations and people cannot defend themselves against measures perceived to be unreasonable. There is no regulated way of protest, complaint or formal appeal.
>
> (Kickert 1991: 26)

From this perspective acquiring a market awareness and the skills of a self-monitoring and individual accountability within the context of 'normal' school activities, would, at least in theory, consolidate the basic principles of self-management within teachers' individual consciousness – decreasing the need for overt control. The individualization of consciousness, oriented towards performativity, constitutes a more subtle yet more totalizing form of control of teachers than is available in the top-down prescriptive steering of state Fordism. Resistance in this context threatens the survival of the institution. It sets the dissenters against the interests of colleagues rather than against policies. Values and interests are thoroughly conflated. And in the use of discretionary payments, loyalty and commitment become criteria for preferment alongside other aspects of 'performance'. While management is being embraced rather than imposed, it is also discursively fostered and privileged via such things as the work of the School Management Task Force and the School Development Plan Project (Hargreaves and Hopkins 1991), and earmarked management training funding.

In all this some decisive shifts are achieved: from public debate to private choice, from collective planning to individual decision making. Together, management and the market remove education from the public arena of civil society, from collective responsibility, and effectively 'privatize' it. The scope and availability of provision are no longer matters of national or local political debate or decision-making. They rest, on the one hand, with consumer choice and competitive individualism and, on the other, with the responsive, entrepreneurial decision making of senior managers in schools. We have the closure and atomization of civil society. In general terms, at the heart of this reforming thrust, what is being attempted is a breakdown of the distinction between public and private goods and the public and private sectors. 'Reformers, in particular, dogmatically assume that public sector management problems are sufficiently similar to those of business to allow the principles of private sector management (if such exist) to be extensively applied' (Metcalfe 1991: 5). This comment and this quotation can be set against an extract from an interview I conducted with a senior DES civil servant in late 1988. It is interesting to reread the interview in the light of such developments as the Parents' Charter, on the one hand, with its prescriptive accountability, and School Development Planning, on the other, with its rhetoric of 'a plan of needs for development set in the context of the school's aims and values, its existing achievement and national LEA policies and initiatives' (DES, 1991a: 2). Possible contradictions between the former and the latter are not contemplated. Moreover, the role of performance indicators in achieving 'steering at a distance' becomes clear here.

CS: We said we're not bothered about what performance indicators you choose, within reason . . . you've got to set the aims and objectives and you've got to monitor whether you're achieving them . . . and you need them not 'cause big brother is going to watch what you're doing, but so that you can manage . . .

SJB: And in turn, I suppose, that feeds back to the whole issue of the way in which schooling is related to the economy. It's a way of ensuring an efficient, effectively related school system, feeding back into the job market.

CS: I am not sure. I think that link might be a bit indirect. I mean that link requires the school to have set as one of its aims or its objectives that it's going to meet the needs of the community.

SJB: But you can make it a form rather than content argument. That the form, the structure which is taken, and things

like appraisal and performance indicators match more
directly with industry, the needs of the economy.

CS: It breaks down this distinction between the way that public
sector things operate and private sector things operate,
doesn't it. To that extent it's reducing the sort of differences between the sectors.

Raab (1991) makes two points about the key role of management
in government education policy, which clearly articulate with these
comments. First, he notes the cultural and value shifts in education
as being part of a more general reform of administration within
government.

> The local management of schools and its attendant functional
> and structural concomitants bear resemblance to the broad
> movement in British government generally of which the effi-
> ciency strategy, decentralisation, performance monitoring,
> management information systems and devolved accountability
> to executive agencies are among the main pillars. This move-
> ment intends to create not just a change in the structures of
> public policy-making and implementation but a cultural revo-
> lution in Whitehall in which public management supplants
> traditional administration.
>
> (Raab 1991: 15)

Second, he underlines the legitimation effect achieved by 'steering
at a distance':

> Government's hope must be that the implantation of the sys-
> tems and ethos of management will take root sufficiently to
> legitimize new mechanisms and routines and to make them
> appear to be self-imposed, or collaboratively adopted, from top
> to toe. In this, headteachers are pivotal, and a massive reaffir-
> mation of their role as managers is being undertaken. Lay
> members of school boards and governing bodies are likewise
> being inducted and trained to a conception of their function
> within a management paradigm of school governance.
>
> (Raab 1991: 16)

In classical Foucauldian terms, as indicated above, we can see
management as a polyvalent discourse. It both liberates and enslaves.
It empowers and subjects. Clearly, devolved budgets have been greeted

by many senior teachers in positive terms – as increasing autonomy and allowing for great flexibility, and as more efficient. 'My power has considerably increased and improved. I am "improved", my colleagues might say "worsened" ' (Headteacher quoted in Halpin *et al.* 1993: 14). (Self-management is discussed more fully in Chapter 5.) The experiences of classroom teachers may be very different. There is an important difference between devolved budgeting and the making of financial policy. LMS has tended to mean that financial policy making rests with a small group of increasingly specialized staff (with small but increasing numbers of them recruited from outside the teaching profession). The training and values and purposes of these specialists are increasingly separating them off from their erstwhile classroom-based colleagues. This deputy head (Flightpath Comprehensive) certainly indicates an awareness of these divisions and the micropolitical tensions they produce.

> I'm worried about this gap that is growing between teachers and teacher management. And it is an 'us and them'. And that is growing, and I can understand why it is growing. It is increasing because of things that are being given to schools to do. It is increasingly becoming a situation where a small group of people at the top, if you can use that phrase, are telling or encouraging, by any methods they can employ – and we're not very experienced managers, we're only people who wanted to become teachers – we're having to use any methods we can to cajole, encourage, other people to actually do things . . . I think with things like LMS – and all these new initiatives just make it worse – is that the actual management initiation of change is being left to a few people who are having to use any strategy they can to change long-established practices among people who are their equal in terms of educational qualifications, certainly experience in many cases.

What this speaker is pointing to is a shift in the form and methods of organizational control in schools and, specifically, the adoption of what Therborn (1978: 54) calls the 'managerial technocratic mode', or what I referred to above as 'generic' management, which is characterized by 'specialization, impersonality and stratified monopolization of intellectual knowledge by professionals'. In other words, we are seeing the emergence of a professionalized cadre of specially trained teacher-managers. This is the basis for a classic

polarization between the values of professional responsibility and
those of efficient management (see Ball and Bowe 1991). It is important that we recognize this polarization as ramifying existing tendencies in school rather than as an entirely new phenomenon.

> It tends to be management and staff, but then it was before. I
> don't think that's changed particularly. Obviously, I've only
> been here since the school became grant-maintained but the
> feeling I got is that it's always been management and staff, and
> the senior team are the senior team and you don't get to hear
> directly about what they're discussing in their meetings.
>
>   (Second year teacher, Martineau School)

Clearly, some senior staff find the reorientations of perspective
required of them by generic management difficult to accept,

> Members of the SMT who have taken the route up straight
> through the teacher grades and are steeped in the history of
> the fifties and sixties, are simply not used to, or don't want to
> work in this way, So there are difficulties in the school because
> of that. But management now in school is a different thing
> from simply overseeing the curriculum.
>
>   (Senior finance and administrative officer,
>   Trumpton School)

But this and other data suggest the development of a division of
values and purposes, of professional culture if you like, between
managers, oriented to the budget, the market, entrepreneurial activities and the drive for efficiency, and teachers, oriented to the
National Curriculum, teaching and learning, student needs and the
drive for effectiveness. Thus, senior teachers find themselves caught
between what they or their colleagues see as the best or proper decision in educational terms and the constraints of the budget or
the market, and thus perhaps institutional survival. There is the
potential for serious value conflicts here. The result is also a set of
keen ethical dilemmas. Both examples again indicate the polyvalent
and productive nature of the management discourse. It constructs
the manager and the manager is captured within it – empowered but
stressed, liberated but anxious. It is paradoxical and double-edged.
Perhaps we should think of the headteacher as a 'state vavasour'.[1]

> My job used to include overseeing the curriculum. Now that
> function has been taken away from me by the National

Curriculum legislation. I'm not overseeing so much as managing an imposed curriculum. That still requires a tremendous amount of work, but it doesn't require an executive function. It is much more management and clerical. At the end of the day, all I am doing is making sure the requirements are being met.

(Headteacher, quoted in Halpin *et al.* 1993: 16)

Within the process and achievement of change, as Raab notes, the ethical and ideological position of the headteacher is crucial. It seems undeniable that the government intended to capture and reconstruct the headteacher as the key actor in the process of reform and redefinition (see Chapter 6). Part of this involves a cultural and structural separating off of the head from the possibility of collegial relations with staff. One aspect of the process of separation and capture is related to pay.

Head teachers' pay would rise by up to 20 per cent if their salaries were put in line with jobs in industry or elsewhere in local authority services, a survey published today by the National Association of Head Teachers' estimates. The association's case, which will be put this autumn to the teachers' pay review body headed by Sir Graham Day, chairman of Rover, is based on analysis by Hay Management Consultants.

(*The Guardian* 19 August 1991)

What we should note here is the context, the points of reference, the framing for the argument. As David Hart, General Secretary of the National Association of Head Teachers, certainly appears to realize, in the context of the ERA, headteachers will be laying claim to a qualitatively different basis for organizational control compared with previously. No longer is this based upon professional authority, but rather 'managerial skill'. He says:

It appears that a 'critical limit' has been reached and that they can no longer rely on the authority of their position to manage their staff. They must have well developed and well rounded managerial skills in order to become effective managers of increasingly complex school environments.

(Hart 1990: 41)

This is part of the articulation of 'managerial power' and the assertion of 'the managerial prerogative' (Storey 1983), which is occurring right across the range of public services in the UK, and elsewhere. Importantly, then, the discourse of management and the appearance of autonomy and self-determination are fed, not only from official sites within government, but also from sites within the domain of practice. In particular, there is now a professional cadre of consultants, writers and advisors who operate to disseminate but also to legitimate management to school managers via a discourse of autonomy and collaboration. By idealizing management as self-management, books like Caldwell and Spinks's (1988) *The Self-managing School* create a professionally acceptable, but unreal, value-free world of consensus, collaboration and self-control. The micropolitics of the school are obliterated or obscured. Differing conceptions of 'what it means to be educated', interest differences, issues related to social justice all disappear from view. The school is sanitized and technicized. There is little evidence of a recognition of 'the gap' in purpose, perspective and values indicated earlier – although Caldwell and Spinks's version of collaboration is based on a firm distinction between policy makers and programme teams. Here, collegial relations, collaboration and participation are colonized by management discourse and purpose (see Chapter 5). As Blackmore (1990: 264) puts it, 'the rhetoric of participatory democracy as it relates to school-based decision-making has been appropriated by "corporate logic".' In these idealized portrayals there is little evidence of conflicts between 'the financial' and 'the educational'. The task of budgeting is simply a matter of costing policies. Planning is clean and professional, unmuddied by ethical dilemmas about image making, self-presentation and market-led planning (see also Angus 1994).

The decontextualized niceties of self-management may apply in certain respects to those schools which are net gainers under their LEA formula, and whose LEA has not found it necessary to cut its general schools budget; but theories and precepts for school organization are needed which also have real relevance to net losers and those for whom autonomy means managing their own cuts. 'All managerial matters are dominated by finding ways of reducing staff, support staff and restricting damage to morale, curriculum, and marketing image' (Head, quoted in Schimell 1991). Like the policies themselves, many of the technical and 'professional' commentaries on school change are written as though all schools were the best of all possible schools. The material and ethical realities of 'making ends meet', of coping with diverse student needs and diverse parental expectations, of low teacher morale, intensification, stress and contradictory policy objectives, are set aside. In this perfect world of rational management and institutional consensus any school which is less than perfect can only see itself as failing or inadequate. It is little wonder that so many school management texts are purchased in hope only to languish on the headteacher's bookshelf. Their only real contribution is to the impression of erudite leadership that they might convey to eagle-eyed visitors.

In many respects the Audit Commission (1991: 20) presents a franker, if less palatable, version of 'collaborative management'.

> Para 41: Although final decisions on a school's development plan rest with the governing body, the Headteacher will take the lead in the preparation of the plan. The Headteacher should involve all the staff who will implement it, *in order to maximise their commitment to its success* (emphasis added).

Here School Development Planning (SDPing) in effect replaces teacher planning with governor/headteacher planning. Teacher participation relates not to involvement for its own sake, as a collegial, professional or democratic concern, but for the purposes of the management of motivation. The SDP signifies and celebrates the exclusion and subjection of the teacher. Not only does the teacher lose control over classroom planning decisions, but will be monitored, judged and compared by criteria set elsewhere. The SDP brings 'the gaze' to bear, the teacher is captured in its thrall.

> Para 48: Having decided on these proposals, the school needs to align its actions to satisfy them. It is not enough to have a planning system which illuminates needs; the school must also 'will the means' to satisfy those needs. Probably choices will need to be made between desirable programmes. Without a school development plan, those choices will be made by default. With a school development plan, *governors can establish between tasks and make explicit decisions about the use of school resources* (emphasis added).
>
> (Audit Commission 1991: 22)

The language here is significant. Teachers, again, are a present absence, they are 'resources' – means to ends. It is interesting to consider what constitutes 'the school'. Here we see how closely the

SDP is tied to the microtechnology of managerial control and is imbricated in the displacement of power and the reconstruction of the teacher's role. As the focus of appraisal, accountability, comparison and review, the teacher is very visible; as an expert professional actor and decision maker she is all but invisible.

Take the DES press release (25 October 1988), 'Partnership: the key to local management of schools':

> Launching a manual of practical advice on LMS – under which most schools will run their own budgets – Mr Butcher said that LMS will stimulate an improvement in the quality of schools' management. *Headteachers, governors, LEAs and parents will all have a crucial role. Headteachers will have powers to match their existing responsibilities – 'a Head is already a manager, of human as well as financial resources, and of the education process as well as the school as an institution'.*

Where are teachers in all this? Again, they are the objects of management relegated to the status of human resources; they do not participate, they are not included in the partnership; they are there *to be managed*. Note, in the quotation earlier from DES Circular 7/ 88, the positioning of teachers as the objects of resource management. They are all but totally excluded from this discursive ensemble, but they are its victims.

It is heads and governing bodies, on the one hand, and client/ parents, on the other, who are empowered by the Education Reform Act. The teacher is caught and crushed in the nexus between management and the market. Teachers are enclosed in 'a web of discourses which sometimes address them, sometimes speak about them, or impose canonical bits of knowledge on them, or use them as a basis for constructing a science that is beyond their grasp – all this together enables us to link an intensification of the interventions of power to a multiplication of discourse' (Foucault 1981: 30). The manager's autonomy becomes the teacher's constraint. Decisions imposed from far away are replaced by decisions imposed from close at hand. It is a common but dire mistake in the literature which celebrates LMS, to take senior manager's comments about great flexibility and freedom under LMS to stand for greater flexibility and freedom for teachers. I quote a senior teacher in one of our case study schools:

It seems to me there are two approaches to LMS. One is to try and maintain education. The message that comes from the senior management to the school is that it is the education of the children that is of paramount importance ... Or you can give the message that we are getting, that everything must be seen in terms of financial implications and therefore we must rethink everything that we do – like when we sit like this, how much is it costing us? Now I feel very uncomfortable about the staff being told over and over again that finance dictates everything.

The reworking of the teacher into a resource (to be managed), a cost calculation, an abstraction increasingly devoid of human qualities, goes further. Brian Knight, writing as guest editor of a special issue of *School Governor*, put forward the following argument in his criticisms of a DES Circular.

Among its shortcomings is that common failure to make the link between school time and school finance. Somehow the myth persists that school finance provides human and physical resources which then create education. It's not true, of course – both resources are unusable until they are converted into 'resource hours'. (If you doubt this, ask how money spent on a computer locked in a cupboard of a teacher left off the timetable makes an impact on the classroom process!) So school time management is that vital interface which converts both resources into usable resources hours.

(Knight 1990: 6)

Again, important discursive work is done here. For the depersonalization and dehumanization of the teacher (the comparison with the computer is significant) as a resource 'to be used' distances managers from the personal and human consequences of their actions.

The possibility of conceptual change outlined above is in part brought about, in part made possible, by the increasing separation of the professional worlds, perspectives and interests of the manager and the teacher. This is especially so when these new worlds are constructed out of discourses which provide concepts and a lexicon which renders people/colleagues into resources and replaces personal relationships with appraisal and commitment with performance incentives.

Conclusion

I recognise that I am painting a grim and, in some respects, a crude picture here. It is crude because the complexities of change in and across schools are partly skated over. It is also crude because it deals almost exclusively with policy texts, rather than with the grassroots interpretation and recreation of policy *in situ*; 'policy initiatives are not unproblematically translated into school practice. Rather they must be mediated through a pre-existing institutional infrastructure, composed of groups and individuals, inscribed within each school's political culture' (Mac an Ghaill 1991: 311). Even so, the reinscription of power relations in education attempted by the ERA offers the potential of a massive over-determination of the work of teaching. In this heterotopia of reform the relationships of teachers with their significant others are changed and confused; the teacher as person and as professional is both scapegoat and victim. Professionality is replaced by accountability, collegiality by costing and surveillance. These are forms of power which are realized and reproduced through social interaction, within the everyday life of institutions. They do not so much bear down upon as take shape within the practices of the institution itself and construct individuals and their social rela-tions through direct interaction. This is, at least in some respects, a positive power, it articulates a mode of personal existence which is inscribed within the 'minute arts of self-scrutiny, self-evaluation, and self regulation' (Rose 1989: 222; see Ball 1990b on teacher appraisal).

> When I think of the mechanics of power, I have in mind rather its capillary form of existence, at the point where power returns into the very grain of individuals, touches their bodies, and comes to insert itself into their gestures and attitudes, their discourses, apprenticeships and daily lives.
>
> (Foucault 1980)

Teachers' careers, institutional micropolitics, and state power and policies are intertwined in a complex process of changes in patterns of control, relationships and values in schools. The meaning of 'the teacher' and the nature of teaching as a career are at stake, as is, in general terms, the future of education as a public service.

Note

1 Vavasours were vassals holding land from a great Lord and having other vassals under them.

5

Cost, culture and control: self-management and entrepreneurial schooling[1]

In Chapter 4 I began to explore the new and invigorated role of management in the 'economy of power' which enmeshes and constitutes teachers. I now want to pursue that analysis further by looking specifically at the notion of the 'self-managing school' (see also Smyth 1993), and the concepts of flexibility and autonomy upon which it rests, and the role played by school development planning in the managerial project.

Management of and in schools, linked to the disciplinary forces of the market and the legal requirements of the National Currriculum, is bringing about a significant transformation of the power relations within which teachers work. The specific tactics of management, set within the general political strategy of educational reform (performativity in particular), related but different and complementary, produce a 'rule' of power which Foucault (1981: 99) calls 'double-conditioning':

> No 'local center', no 'pattern of transformation' could function if, through a series of sequences, it did not eventually enter into an over-all strategy. And inversely, no strategy could achieve comprehensive effects if it did not gain support from precise and tenuous relations serving, not as its point of application or final outcome, but as its prop and anchor point.

Thus, I argue that the discourse of 'management' is a key feature of the current reform of education. In a variety of ways it articulates a new culture of schooling, a culture of commodification and output indicators which articulates with the culture of choice and relative advantage into which parents are being drawn. Concomitantly, the market both empowers and transforms the work of school management. The devolution of school budgets; the greatly reduced powers of LEAs; the break-up of national pay agreements for teachers; and the encouragement given to entrepreneurial innovation and income generation; all contribute to an illusion of autonomy and flexibility for the manager. Together the market and the management reforms replace collective, bureaucratic controls, structures and relationships with individualistic and competitive ones. Schools are inserted into a new paradox; they are to be given greater autonomy within the constraints and pressures of market forces; they are to be able to exercise flexibility in order to be more responsive. The relative certainties of local democracy and beaucracy are to be replaced by the relative uncertainties of enrolment-based funding. The point about both management and the market is that they are 'no hands' forms of control as far as the relationship between education and the state is concerned – thus management is transformed into self-management with all the semantic and ideological confusion that that brings with it. As discussed in Chapter 4, management and the market provide in Kickert's (1991) terms 'steering at a distance'.

> The Education Reform Act of 1988 and recent legislation aim to raise levels of pupil achievement in particular through the introduction of the National Curriculum and improved self-management by schools.
>   For governors, Headteachers and teachers, bringing together these changes will require, as part of the new partnership, strategies for managing development and change to make schools more effective. School Development Plans are a means of realising this goal.
>
> (DES 1989: 4)

Self-management is key to the achievement of 'steering at a distance', it articulates self-regulation with a microtechnology of control and ramifies the value and cultural changes set in train by finance-led decision making and competition. In other words, it is a disciplinary practice. But as a discourse, management is productive rather than simply coercive. It increases the power of individuals – managers and managed in some respects – while making them more docile. Management is both a body of precepts, assumptions and theory, to be learned by managers, and a set of practices to be implemented, encompassing both managers and managed. It is in Foucault's terms an 'infinitesimal mechanism' of power with its own history and trajectory and tactics. And it is such power relations at the micro-level of society which make possible certain global effects of domination. This is a microphysics of oppression, not, that is, the long and coercive arm of the state at work but a bottom-up capillary process of local and unstable relations. This is a set of power relations which are produced 'from one moment to the next, at every point', which are self-reproducing, immanent. This power is not a thing that is possessed but practices that are 'exercised'. And while 'the logic is perfectly clear, the aims decipherable . . . there is none there to have invented them' (Foucault 1979: 95).

But management itself (as theory/as practice) is not of a piece. It is not a unitary perspective. There are at least two, perhaps three, discourses of management in play here within the reform process in the UK. They have different effects. One is what might be called 'professional management'. This is articulated around a development planning perspective and relates particularly to the production of school management plans – 'The purpose of development planning is to improve the quality of teaching and learning in a school through the successful management of innovation and change' (Hargreaves and Hopkins 1991: 3)(H and H). Three things should be noted about this discourse at the outset: (a) it provides a vocabulary which links management directly to classroom practice; (b) it articulates with a teacherly 'professional' perspective on planning and purpose; (c) it starts from a concern with managing change.

> We believe that when heads and governors see LMS as a spur
> to development planning (of which financial management is a
> component), they have taken a road to what will truly be 'self-
> managing schools' – ones which not merely learn to manage
> change and finance but also learn the art of school improve-
> ment which leads to more effective teaching and learning.
>
> (Hargreaves and Hopkins 1991: 13)

A bold statement of faith! In many ways this is the acceptable face of management. Inasmuch as it begins from the professional end of the planning spectrum, it is 'clean' (context-free) management insofar as it treats the school in isolation and concentrates upon the business of *education* rather than education as *business*. The H and H book has only one index entry for finance. This approach is very process-oriented, it is a value-free, content-free management (in the sense that good practice is entirely a matter of process). It is the management of anything or nothing (and this is profoundly disturbing). It divorces management practices from values and from politics. The H and H book has only one index entry for values. It is technically oriented, rational and apolitical. There are no index entries in the H and H book for conflict. This is management in the best of all possible schools. It is anodyne and reassuring and does a great deal to legitimate management to the professional audience.

The second discourse I would term 'financial management'. It begins from a concern with balancing the books, with maximizing the budget, and with doing educationally what can be afforded. This is for many practitioners the unacceptable face of management – but, I would argue, a very real 'on the ground' approach. It is driven by context, by the realities of per capita funding, 'rate-capping' (government imposed limits on local government spending) and competition with neighbouring schools (see below). This is in stark contrast to the Mary Poppins world (a spoonful of sugar . . .) of management conjured up by 'professional management' texts like Caldwell and Spinks (1988) (C and S). In Caldwell and Spinks's five-point programme for planning and budgeting in collaborative school management the cost of plans is only mentioned in item 4: 'identifying and costing resources required in the plan for implementation'. This is a far cry from the 'what we can afford' world of cuts in public sector spending which most schools currently find themselves in. And there are no entries for either competition or marketing in the C and S index.

There is a close relationship between the discourse of financial management and the third management discourse, which I call 'entrepreneurial management'. Here the market is to the fore; image, hype and PR, and competition, diversification and income generation are prominent in the managers' lexicon.

Stanley Goodchild [at the time head of Garth Hill School in Berkshire] was quoted as saying that 'we see the school very much as a business – where the business is educating young people'. Alternatively, he said in the press release (sent out prior to the press conference at which Alan Watts was introduced to reporters):

We are sitting on a valuable resource which is not being used to full effect. If we are able to provide a service for local industry and commerce and at the same time increase the resource available for our students then I would be a very foolish Head not to take advantage.

Press releases; press conferences – this is a new deal for state education.

Press Release. Royal County of Berkshire. Date 4th September 1986. No. 919.

BUSINESS MANAGER APPOINTED AT BERKSHIRE SCHOOL Alan Watts who has spent his lifetime in senior management private industry, is next Monday (September 14) becoming what is believed to be the first ever Business manager at a local authority school.

(Goodchild and Holly 1989: 246)

This third version is both the product and mechanism of what Keat (1991: 5) calls 'cultural engineering'. He says:

The task of constructing an 'enterprise' culture is (at least) twofold . . . First, a wide range of institutions and activities must be remodelled along the lines of the commercial enterprise, including its orientation to the demands of the consumer. Second, the acquisition and exercise of enterprising qualities must be encouraged, so that the increasingly commercialised world will itself take on an appropriately 'enterprising' form.

Version 3 is most influenced by the values of enterprise and business but experience of version 2 is not unlike the real world of business, especially in the context of economic recession. In some ways, version 2, the financial, is closer to a corporate or 'big business' perspective, based on speed of decision making, cost improvement, coordination and accountability. Version 3 is closer to a 'small business' perspective, based upon market criteria, pricing and competition.

Clearly, in practice these discourses are not mutually exclusive, although their mixing is not easily achieved in every case. There are contradictions in principle, orientation and practice between versions 1 and 2, and in ethos and method between versions 1 and 3. The problem is that version 1 is not infrequently used to idealize the real use of versions 2 and 3. In a sense, version 1 is a 'science of the abstract' and versions 2 and 3 are 'sciences of the concrete' (Hatton 1988: 341). The differences between these versions cannot be reduced to matters of emphasis. And each version is supported and legitimated by a different set of texts. H and H and C and S are perhaps the key texts for version 1. Version 2 is underpinned by a set of technical manuals concerned with budgetary control, which tend not to be integrated with or cross-referenced to versions 1 and 3. An example of a version 3 entrepreneurial text is provided by Fidler and Bowles's *Effective Local Management of Schools* (1989). Here the relationship of management to planning and to organizational aims is very different from that envisaged by H and H. Marketing professionals, Fidler and Bowles (1989: 38) argue,

> would insist that marketing should be seen as integral to the management role of any enterprise operating in a competitive environment and be a total strategy starting from the aims and objectives of the organisation, feeding into its information and decision-making systems and being closely connected to monitoring, evaluation and staff development activities.

In this conception of the manager and of the organization's relationship to the market, 'professional' judgements are regarded with profound suspicion. The 'mission statement' of the organization begins not with principles but 'by establishing clearly whose needs the school is there to serve. It has been too producer-dominated, too concerned with serving its own ends and imposing its own views on its clients. The present changes are designed to make the system more responsive, more answerable to the customer' (Fidler and Bowles 1989: 40). Within this vision of the school, management mediates between a production technology and the customer. The manager's concerns relate to external quality control and internal cost control. The professionality so centrally positioned in the H and H and C and S texts is decentred here. Teaching and learning are defined by customers' needs, not by professional planning or judgement (although market-related funding might not have this effect in all schools – see below). The aim is to drive out all the 'natural ambiguities' which inhere in public service provision in complex and controversial areas like education (and health).

Now it might be argued that these discourses/versions of management should be seen as different aspects of the role of management in the school – allocated to different members of the senior management team or different aspects of the headteacher's total workload. But that is too simple. The values and cultures of institutions differ. The role and leadership styles attempted by heads differ, they are inflected and biased differently. Schools differ in terms of the extent to which any of these discourses become dominant and pervasive. The possibilities here are very much related to a school's history and market position. However, few schools will be able to think about or organize themselves without use of or reference to these lexicons of control. As I have tried already to indicate, the reform process in the UK is not simply structural or technical – it is also cultural and ideological. On the one hand, as we shall see, management as practice is unstable and complex: 'Its success is proportional to its ability to hide its own mechanisms' (Foucault 1979: 86). But, on the other hand, as a discourse of power and control, management is both a sophisticated technology and a pervasive commonsensical perspective.

Management is both means and end in the reform process. That is to say, management (as synonym for efficiency) is taken to be 'the one best way' to organize and run schools, and to the extent that management embraces enterprise and commercialism it shifts schools away from the 'culture of welfare' towards the 'culture of profit and production' – that is, management does profound ideological work in relation to the conception and conduct of schooling. It is an end in itself. But management and most particularly self-management is also seen as a way of delivering other changes. It is a mechanism for ensuring the delivery of a National Curriculum, and it ties classroom practice, student performance, teacher appraisal, school recruitment and resource allocation into a single tight bundle of planning and surveillance. It gives apparent autonomy to the manager while taking apparent autonomy away from the teacher. It drives a wedge between the curriculum- and classroom-oriented teacher and the market- and budget-oriented manager, thus creating a strong potential for differences in interest, values and purpose between the two groups. This gap is vividly present across our research on educational reform. The experience of this gap, the reworking of relationships within or across it, are subtle aspects of resocialization for those on both sides (see below).

The work of management in the resocialization of the managers and the managed and the construction of new roles and relationships for and between them is basic to the reform process and the

achievement of new forms of control. The forms of self-management
currently in play politically and textually are discursively distinct from
either notions of empowerment (NASSP Bulletin 1991) or interactive rationality (Saltman and Von Otter 1992). Self-management is
the panopticon of modern educational organization.

Practising management

The scenario of change outlined thus far now needs some elabora-
tion. Two points have to be made. First, there are a whole set of implications for organizational culture and relationships stemming from
the professionalization of school management as self-management.
Second, the rhetorics of reform, in articulating a key role for management, idealize and misrepresent the new freedoms and possibilities of devolution and school-based management. Using Kickert's
terms, in both the political rhetoric and the money-spinning system of publishing and consultancy which supports, legitimizes and
disseminates self-management, the 'distance' is stressed and the
'steering' is played down. These idealizations need to be carefully
deconstructed and the rhetorics of school development planning,
financial management and entrepreneurship need to be tested
empirically against the practice of management. Self-management
in schools is being developed in the nexus between flexibility and
constraint, autonomy and response. The political and professional
literature attends primarily to flexibility and autonomy and has little
to say about responsiveness and constraint.

Culture and relationships

Two major interrelated factors are evident in the 'new' cultural climate
of UK schools. First, there is a clear division or 'gap' developing
between school managers, oriented primarily to matters of financial
planning, income generation and marketing, and classroom practitioners, oriented primarily to the demands of the National Curriculum
and National Testing. Notions like collaborative planning (C and S)
ideologically paper over the significance of such divisions. But this is
a 'gap' of values, purposes and perspective.

In discussions I've found that I was looking at the gap from the
senior manager point of view. And I think there's another whole
way of looking at it [from the point of view of teaching staff]

that they themselves should be now, and increasingly will in the future be having to appreciate some of the management issues we are facing. The gap is on both sides in other words.

(Headteacher, Flightpath Comprehensive,
research discussion day)

One deputy head in our research schools captured the essence of the change in orientation that he was caught up in, when he explained: 'The Education Reform Act . . . has really shifted the focus of the management team . . . from managing education to managing an educational institution' (Senior deputy, Parkside Comprehensive). In other words, he now found himself operating as a generic manager with increasingly less of an educational orientation and with 'recourse to universalistic concepts of the efficient management of organizations in difficult circumstances' (Spybey 1984: 550). He went on: 'all my non-teaching, non-contact time is taken up with going to meetings, or meeting people and organizing things, concerned with finance and resources, and not with promoting the grassroots educational programme of the school.' Within this 'gap', this division of purposes and interests, there is considerable potential for tension and conflict, particularly in direct confrontations between financial planning and educational judgements about good practice (see Ball and Bowe 1991).

I am a very practical person, and whilst the theory of education is all very well, as far as I'm concerned, unless you can put it into practice, then it isn't of great value . . . and I have certainly been torn between those roles. Of wanting to get in and really have the power to make the final decisions, and really retain my close links and the respect of staff, because its very easy with the rapid change in the curriculum, to forget how difficult it is to be in the classroom. Staff that have been out of classroom teaching for the last five years could not easily understand the pressures that young staff are under – which some of them find very difficult to cope with. And it's very easy to lose touch with what's going on if you're not careful. You have to make a very conscious effort to retain that awareness.

(Deputy head, Flightpath Comprehensive)

In these situations the 'steering at a distance' aspects of reform and the role of management in the 'delivery' of performativity are clear within the microphysics of the institution. The manager, in

effect, stands for and does the work of the state in imposing financial
limits and disciplines in the practices of colleagues. The development of a school management plan is the key tactical device for
mobilizing and imposing self-management across and through the
organization – for achieving change and asserting control.

> What we've decided to do is hold seven open meetings from
> February onwards, but there's this anxiety in the senior man-
> agement committee about how the staff are going to respond
> to it. There will be six meetings on each of the main thrusts of
> the SMP, plus finance. But it's interesting to look at what the
> head has put down as what these meetings will seek to do –
> 'provide an opportunity for staff to develop planning strategies
> with quantifiable achievable objectives in a timespan of one to
> five years'. The implication is that the SMP is in place, you
> need to know its in place, so you now have to think about
> quantifying what you're doing. The next thing, raise questions
> about the school's aims and purposes in a year of unparalleled
> change imposed by government legislation with far-reaching
> implications for the future. That's admitting what we said ear-
> lier, that the aims and purposes, in a sense, have been trivialized
> in this whole exercise.
>
> (Senior deputy, Flightpath Comprehensive)

Here, then, performativity is the cutting edge of the planning
process, the plan is 'an effect' rather than a process, aims are subordinate to an externally imposed agenda (and financial limits). But
this school is struggling to take seriously the mechanisms of reform.
On the one hand, the senior management committee has produced
an SMP. And the head intends that this will provide the basis of
objectives setting and target setting within the school – it will become
a disciplinary instrument. All this is recognized as being instrumental
rather than purposeful. That is to say, the plan is an instrument of
management rather than a representative of collectively discussed
aims and purposes, which have been 'trivialized'. As the deputy says
earlier in the same interview, 'we put the cart before the horse in
bunging through this management plan'. On the other hand, the
senior managers are clearly worried about the response of the teachers. And embedded in this worry is a new uncertainty about the roles
and relationships of teachers and managers. Later in the same interview he said, 'the whole question of whether you over-burden people

or patronise them is a major problem' (see Wallace 1991, on the role of SDPs in the reform process). This *realeconomik* gives a particular thrust and intonation to the work of the self-managers.

The relationship between financial planning and the educational technology of the institution, although mediated by management, is ultimately constrained by the vicissitudes of the market and national and local government budget setting.

> I think there's no doubt at all that the finance and the quantitative approach is very much in the picture. I've always tried to keep it no more than in the middle ground. I don't think that the school should be driven purely by finance. If the school has stable numbers or slightly increasing numbers, I can see we can maintain that position, an almost idealistic position if you like. But I can see that once the school starts going into decline, then it is finance that is going to determine the quality of the product. But while we are stable I'd like to see us maintaining the quality as opposed to the quantity of education.
>
> (Senior deputy, Parkside Comprehensive)

A further element of the cultural gap between managers and teachers anticipates the discussion of flexibility and responsiveness later. That is, the extent to which teachers' practice is oriented to the immediate needs of students becomes an aspect of the way the school markets itself to clients (see also Handscomb 1992), i.e. whether practice is driven by professional judgement or market forces. In this tension, the manager is caught between the client and the practitioner. This reorientation of the managers and the potential for distancing from the more immediate classroom concerns of teachers can be gauged from the following examples of new market relations in schools. They also point up the ideological and cultural changes produced within the current reform process. One of our research schools has obtained a commercial loan to build a sports hall (which includes a bar):

> with the express aim of it being available to the community, as a self-financing, hopefully, even profit-making enterprise. We are having to create a market for the use of this. And that's why I spent last Sunday on site as licensee of the bar, from twelve o'clock to three o'clock and found that the total takings for that period was £4.28. We'd nowhere near covered the cost of the barmaid or the other people who were on site. It's in the

classic position of any small business that is starting up. You lose money the first year or two years, before you start breaking even and making a profit.

And there are a whole range of facilities the school's got that are quite marketable, if you can create a market for them. There is the languages department, who can make their services available to local industry for 1992 and all that in terms of the European market. Or IT equipment for running courses and so on. It's a completely new culture and it involves a certain amount of retraining of educationalists if you were to go down that road.

(Headteacher, Flightpath Comprehensive)

The second example is similar:

It may well be that ultimately we'll get a different form of spending and we'll also be funded more on an industrial basis . . . which takes us to another area, which is income generation, which we now regard as essential. Especially the 9.2 acres we've just been given and the development of that for recreational purposes. I'm contacting various people to see if we can raise sponsorship or loans to make that an all-weather surface, which we can let out and generate income from. But in going into the marketplace like that, we have to make sure that we are in an area of the market which can guarantee income for many years to come.

(Senior deputy, Parkside)

In effect, for the self-managers of the school, security and stability, and thus survival, are beginning to become culturally and organizationally founded upon and oriented to issues related to income generation (from both student enrolments and elsewhere) rather than the production process itself – teaching and learning. And security, stability and survival cannot be simply equated with responsiveness. It is not axiomatic that the market does, or can, produce responsiveness, especially when the impact of individual consumers on the well-being of the whole institution is minimal. 'Whether publicly accountable or market-driven, large organizations contain inherent pressures to pursue their own internal objectives and self-interest in lieu of meeting what are diverse and often diffuse consumer needs' (Saltman and Von Otter 1992: 99–100).

Flexibility and autonomy

Much of the rhetoric of devolution and school-based management rests on a celebration of the new freedoms available to individual schools, to take control of their own futures, to make their own decisions about the distribution and use of their own resources – leaving aside the question of who experiences greater autonomy or gets to exercise greater flexibility. The question of autonomy and flexibility also has to be set in relation to the constraints of the education market, to cuts in funding and to the introduction of a National Curriculum. When the limitations and constraints involved here are taken into account autonomy may be less real than apparent. Heads may find themselves with a new, more demanding role, new, more difficult staff, governor and parent relationships, and a lot of new responsibilities but little new freedom or power (see Arnott *et al.* 1992). The following comments appear to deploy 'responding' as a key concept in expressing the feelings and experiences of headship.

> I don't feel that I lead the way I used to. I'm responding. I'm responding to the national curriculum. I'm also responding to the LEA and they seem to be running like mad . . . we seem to be inundated with inspections and pressures that are coming through the LEA. My role has changed drastically. The main interest used to be curriculum innovation. Now I just run around servicing everybody else.
>
> (Headteacher, Overbury Comprehensive)

Here the headteacher seems to be on the receiving end of the reform process, its instrument rather than its agent. Her role is significantly changed as a result. Again the contradictions within the reform agenda and the over-determination of the school are evident. This is a belt and braces, carrot and stick reform strategy. Another example:

> Now it strikes me that what has happened in the last two or three years is that whatever equilibrium you had established as a head, has now been disturbed by the sheer volume of stuff that is coming around, and one is actually responding to whole sets of initiatives and it is not until we are actually, as heads of institutions, able to stand back and regain some sense of that equilibrium and well being that the institution as a whole will benefit.
>
> (Headteacher, Parkside Comprehensive)

And more specifically a deputy head:

> the kind of conflict that we suspected early on would emerge
> between a thrusting National Curriculum, that is broad and
> balanced and all the rest of it, and the kind of things that
> schools actually do for certain pupils which allow them to go
> off at tangents, is there. And I feel that this is a genuine con-
> flict. I don't think I'm attacking the National Curriculum, I'm
> actually saying the National Curriculum is focusing on something
> that in the next few years will become increasingly problematic.
>   (Flightpath Comprehensive)

It is tempting to suggest that these indications of an absence of
'real' autonomy point up the disciplinary role of self-management.
*That is to say, self-management is a mechanism for delivering reform rather
than a vehicle for institutional initiative and innovation.* Certainly, here
again the 'steering capacity' of the state is evident. But it is important to set the comments above against others which indicate the ways
in which school managers *do* have a new sense of control, particularly in relation to financial flexibility. We should not forget, however,
that this flexibility is achieved at the cost of others' conditions of
work and pay; the replacement of fully trained with less well qualified teachers; teachers with auxiliaries, full-time teachers with part-
time or short-term contract staff.

> I wouldn't be giving away extra incentive allowances because
> we haven't got the money to do it. And I wouldn't know where
> it would come from unless we turned the gas off or whatever.
> But even within the limited money that you've got, the flexibility
> of LMS has helped enormously, in that we have been able to
> take our head of library and put in an extra teaching day, with
> a point 2 allowance, for someone else, in order to enable her
> to develop learning resources, and appoint a learning resources
> assistant and appoint someone two days a week in the office . . .
>   (Headteacher, Pankhurst Comprehensive)

We're only 1 per cent down this year because we are cushioned. Now I love this word cushioned, next year we will have
to lose between 2 and 3 per cent again. Had we had to take the
real LMS shortfall we would have been £60,000 short. But
nevertheless there is flexibility there. You see, if you've got *x*
amount of pounds for a learning resource assistant, then either

you can add to it and have a sort of resources person on £16,000 a year or you say we'll have someone on grade 2 or 3.

(Headteacher, Overbury Comprehensive)

In the school as a whole we've got more than 20 people doing short-term contracts or supply cover, things like that. All these cost savings are quite important.

(Senior Deputy, Parkside)

Again, the heads and deputies quoted here were not unaware of the cost dimension of their planning *as a constraint*, nor of the tensions between a financial agenda based upon the most efficient use of resources and an educational agenda related to effectiveness in terms of student learning (for example, in terms of school size). (And crucially again flexibility is described and explained here in financial terms. The financial discourse is asserting itself as the predominant discourse of school organization.) The thrust of the Conservative government's commitment to the market is that 'successful' schools grow (although the scheme to fund the expansion of such schools was short-lived): all schools are funded primarily on numbers of students enrolled. Concerns about the relationship between school size or class size and educational effectivity therefore play little role in this unit-cost approach to school finance.

I would probably say that half the size would be more effective in those terms [educational] but the reality is that you've got a large capital resource and the costs within that mean that you must operate nearer your maximum capacity to be cost effective. But the quality of the broader education may not be as good as one would like it to be.

(Headteacher, Flightpath)

Peter Downes, a headteacher with long experience of devolved budget-holding, recently produced an article which points up two rather different aspects of devolved financial management. The first is coping with cuts. Cambridgeshire LEA proposed cuts amounting to between £30,000 and £80,000 per school, per year.

The prospect of cuts of this size has come as a shock to Cambridgeshire Heads. As many of us have been managing our own budgets for nearly a decade, most of the possible savings have already been made. Zero expenditure on books, equipment and materials is totally unrealistic. If anything, heads of department are looking for increased funding as they re-equip for the national curriculum.

(Here is an example of two aspects of policy colliding within the remit of management – see below.) But Downes goes on to argue that at least the devolution of budgets provides insights into how budgets are constructed and allocated, insights which were previously unobtainable.

> By introducing LMS, the Government has opened the door of the secret garden of education finance. It can never be shut again. Heads or governors who now have the unenviable task of implementing difficult financial decisions imposed on them from afar, ought, I believe, to mount a campaign for access to central government financial information in a comprehensible format.

Conclusions

As indicated above, one of the ideological and discursive tricks that self-management achieves is that a great deal of fundamental change (in teachers' work and workplace relationships, in decision making processes, in the linking of reward closely to performance, in the disciplining of classroom practice) is not now seen as being done *to* schools but done *by* schools (with the proviso that it is in reality one group of people in schools managing another group). The school, the manager, the teacher and the student are all and each measured and compared by their performance, their output. They are rewarded or punished accordingly.

The key points of control here are over the discourse of self-management and over the indicators of performance, rather than over practice (although, as indicated above, other aspects of reform attempt to intervene directly into practice). Both, and particularly the latter, are subject to state control; the indicators of performance are the mechanisms of steering by the state (see 1993 Education Act and Parents' Charter 1991). The other fundamental transference achieved by 'steering at a distance' is that once the rhetoric of devolution is accepted then it becomes possible to blame the schools for the faults and difficulties inherent in or created by the policies. This is crucial. Parental choice and market schooling provide two avenues for the displacement of the legitimation crisis in education. The state can distance itself from problems in education by blaming parents for making bad or ill-informed choices and by blaming schools for poor self-management, the misuse of their new autonomy. The schools are left to deal with the contradictions that policies create. All too often in policy research and in the texts of self-management the focus of attention is entirely upon the strengths and weaknesses, faults and difficulties of individual schools. The role of policy makers within the state in creating dilemmas and contradictions with which schools must deal is ignored. The state is left in the enviable position of having power without responsibility.

The uneasy professional double-bind created by this kind of policy nexus is nowhere more acute than when – as in the UK setting presently – devolution is accompanied by reductions in education budgets (see above). Schools find themselves 'starved of cash and playing with pennies', as one headteacher put it. It is tempting to see the devolution of budgets and self-management as ways of getting those being cut to cut themselves and to think that it is for the best because they control their own decline. There is a shift of institutional focus from the cuts themselves to the ways of coping with cuts: a shift to dealing with what you can control rather than what you cannot. And if the alternative is that someone else would control your decline then this may be the best of a bad job. But massive work of ideological and social control is done in the meantime. And the ideological role of self-management in relation to the state is never more clear-cut.

Self-management provides a framework for a new institutional culture and for a process of resocialization; it interpollates a new kind of headteacher – although it is difficult to believe that there is a wholesale, unproblematic shift of subjectivity going on among senior teachers – but none the less the new conditions and discourses of consciousness do construct new forms of consciousness and new patterns and possibilities of career. Mike Davies, Co-Director of Stantonbury Campus, writes about the new culture and its effects:

new teachers and those looking towards the furtherance of their career see that the 'top' jobs involve management activity, then it is hardly surprising that staffroom conversation is about management, systems and procedures, rather than about the excitement of the last lesson and the looking forward to the

next. The ubiquitous way in which money and financial consideration can dominate management is a real coup for a government determined to stratify the system and deny that schools
are for radical social change.

(Davies 1992: 5)

What Davies indicates is the potential profundity of the reform
process, and the key role of self-management again in those reforms.
The dominant reality of the school as an organization, at least for its
leaders and managers, is shifted and reconstructed. And we should
bear in mind Foucault's key point that within microtechnologies of
control (like self-management) those who exercise power are just as
much captured and shaped as are those over whom power is wielded.

> In this form of management, power is not totally entrusted to
> someone who would exercise it alone, over others, in an abso-
> lute fashion, this machine is one in which everyone is caught,
> those who exercise power as well as those who are subjected
> to it.
>
> (Foucault 1977: 156)

Davies again:

> I cannot believe that hundreds of Headteachers, whose profes-
> sional and job satisfaction has come through working with
> teachers and children so that they can walk along the road
> towards empowerment and liberty, can so quickly swop all this
> for the keyboard, spreadsheet and bank balance. Post '88, we
> seem to have entered a new era of managerialism without ever
> being clear what it is that we are managing. It may be over
> simplistic to characterise the many dimensions of the Head-
> teacher's role into two giant ledgers, but if we take one sub-
> stantive column relating to being the 'leading professional' and
> the other being 'the managing director', then so much of our
> re-orientation since the end of the last decade has led us to
> serving the mythical customer with an insatiable appetite for
> statistics and league tables and providing information for the
> Board of Governors.
>
> (Davies 1992: 2)

Again this highlights the headteacher as both beneficiary and victim
of reform, both in and out of control. The head is freed and constrained within the management role, as well as being subject to

other forms of control, as indicated above. Again the conceptual and empirical simplicities of the devolution and school-based management literature (Caldwell and Spinks 1989) are pointed up. Indeed, it might be more appropriate to conceptualize school managers not as more autonomous than before but as having been recast as 'the agents of central Whitehall control', as Cousins (1987) and Widgery (1988) argued is the case in the National Health Service, with the result that education is both much less subject to local democratic controls and generally part of a more 'state-centric' system of public services.

The textual apologists of self-management provide a professionalization and legitimation of self-subjugation in articulating an idealized technology for reworking the cultural and interpersonal dynamics of schooling. These texts are firmly imbricated in the construction of new forms of control and concomitantly the reconstruction of teachers' subjectivities, relationships and careers, and thus also the possibilities of their efficacy and autonomy. The discourses to which they contribute are complex and polyvalent, empowering and disempowering, intersecting and contradictory.

Note

1 This chapter reworks, extends and develops ideas outlined in Ball (1990d, 1992a), Ball and Bowe (1991) and Bowe and Ball with Gold (1992). It is based on a symposium paper given at the 1992 AERA Conference, San Francisco and was published previously in Smyth, J. (1993) *A Socially Critical View of the Self-managing School*, London, Falmer.

6

'New headship' and school leadership: new relationships and new tensions

School leadership is not, as some writers on school management would have us believe, achieved in a social vacuum (Angus 1994). The realization of leadership is always set within a framework of possibilities and constraints derived from educational policy and from the political and economic context of education. I am not suggesting that school leaders never have freedom for manoeuvre – there is always room for nuanced interpretations of policy and local concerns and there are institutional variations in the material pressures faced by leaders – but the policy framework will articulate particular leadership roles and responsibilities and exclude others (see Davies 1992, quoted in Chapter 5). One crucial aspect of this articulation is the way in which policies affect and constrain the relationships within which leadership is realized; relationships, that is, with significant others in the institution and its environment.

It is this issue of relationships that I want to take up in looking at the current development of 'new headship' roles in England and Wales. In doing so I will concentrate specifically on the roles of secondary school headteachers.

If we begin with the primary policy framework; this is set by the provisions of the 1986 Education Act and the 1988 Education Reform Act. The latter is complex and comprehensive but I would want to emphasize four aspects of it. (1) The formal powers of governance in schools now rest with the elected/appointed governing body. Formally at least the institutional autonomy of the head is reduced. Deem (1990: 168) explains:

Much of the research on governing bodies, then, suggests that prior to the 1986 Act a skilful Head could manipulate governors, feeding them selected bits of information and pushing them into supportive roles whether this was what the governors wanted or not. But the 1986 and 1988 Acts make this more difficult. Governors now not only have wider responsibilities defined in law but may potentially, as LMS and the National Curriculum get under way, be taken to court for failing to exercise those responsibilities in accordance with the law.

(2) With the introduction of LMS, heads now, on behalf of their governing body, exercise primary day-to-day control of and virement over the school budget. (3) Given the heads/governor's control over budgets, appointments, contracts, promotions and incentive awards, heads are now *de facto* employers of teachers. (4) Given that budgets are primarily derived from student numbers and that parents have open choice of schools for their children, heads are now in a market-driven, client/consumer relationship with parents. Thus, all of the immediate key relationships which affect and construct the possibilities of headship and school leadership – relationships with governors, the teachers and parents – are now changed. This is the context of what I refer to as 'new headship'. (There are also changes in Headteachers' relationships with the local education authority.)

Having pointed up these changes, I do not want to give the impression that these new relationships are clear and unequivocal and that as a result the constraints and possibilities of leadership in this new policy context are clear and unequivocal. There are very significant changes taking place in the roles of headteachers but these changes only serve to highlight the uncertainties and disturbing lack of clarity produced by recent legislation. There is an underlying lack of clarity relating to the 'new headship' in general terms – and the definition of the Headteacher's role and powers – and a set of specific issues that remain unclear, which relate to each of the key relationships I have identified. It is to these I now turn.

The general and underlying issue, which thereby affects all else, is the question of whether the changes brought about by the 1988 Act should be understood as articulating headship in terms of a new flexibility and autonomy or whether they actually construct a new but less obvious and immediate set of constraints upon headship (see Chapter 5). The political rhetorics associated with these policy

changes unequivocally stress the former but the experiences of at
least some Headteachers point to the latter (Arnott *et al.* 1992). The
emphasis on flexibility derives from: the much reduced possibilities
of LEA influence over school policies; the head's budgetary autonomy;
the increased latitude available to the head in relation to teachers'
national pay structures and the increased possibility of the use of
part-time and short-term contracts; the new emphasis on income
generation; and the removal of most LEA controls over catchment
areas and school recruitment. But almost all of these sources of
greater flexibility have a flipside of new constraints. The LEA influence
over school policies is replaced by a legally required National Curriculum; budgets relate to enrolment (which can of course go up
or down in the new market of parental choices) but are ultimately
dependent upon the overall level of government spending on education and the general schools budget set by each LEA (the size of
these varies considerably). Thus, schools can find themselves with
more students, having more efficient and effective use of available
resources and still less money than previously. Further, the time,
energy and attention that headteachers now devote to the budget,
income generation and public relations and the new employer/
employee relationship with teaching (and other) staff (more of which
below) can seriously diminish the possibility of the head's educational leadership role in the school. And, finally, in the new educational market place 'bureaucratic' constraints upon decision making
in the school are replaced by the constraints of consumer preference
and the demands of government-imposed measures and indicators
of performance. It may be that flexibility is more apparent than real,
or trivial rather than substantial. We can explore this more concretely
by moving on to the specifics outlined above. The rest of the chapter
will focus on the current 'possibilities' of school headship via an
examination of the new relationships of leadership. I want to illustrate these, and the problems arising from them, with data drawn
from research.

Leadership, governance and policy

Writing in 1990, Deem (p. 168) commented that: 'It is unclear at
present whether Headteachers will continue to dominate governing
bodies in the way that they did prior to the new legislation. Certainly
Headteachers have often viewed governors either with disdain or as

part of a necessary but relatively unimportant ritual in the past.' That lack of clarity remains. As suggested already, the lack of clarity about working relationships between heads and governors and thus the possibilities of the head's leadership in the school is not one simply of developing new practices: it is embedded in the legislation.

First, I quote Mr Green, headteacher of Flightpath Comprehensive. Mr Green is keen to erect and maintain a separation between what he calls governance, the role of governors, and management, the role of senior managers in the school and preordinately the head. But he fears that this separation is all too easily breached.

> There is some movement, some trend for governors, particularly in primary schools, and maybe in some secondary, to be more involved with management issues than governance issues. And it is very easy to start setting up [as many schools have done] sub-committees of governing bodies that mirror management structures and once you start doing that you begin to get your lines of decision-making confused ... [Senior managers] have the continuity through their involvement with the school, that governors may not, that the parent governors and other governors may not. They have the experience and background in educational issues and the educational world, that governors wouldn't have. They have the ability to sift and understand complex papers on policy matters ... The stronger the head, the senior management team, the greater the risk [of them manipulating and dominating the governors]. And of course you can have the tables turn the other way round, where the governors are very strong, very interventionist, and management very weak. Then this can make a school unmanageable. Governors through governance, do in fact make it unmanageable. And they are areas that concern me enormously, particularly within primary schools, where there is less experience, governors there may be far more interventionist than they should be and senior managers will allow them because they are educationalists at heart, teachers at heart.

This, of course, is only one side of the story, the view from the head. The questions are how, in practice, 'intervention' is defined by head and governors and whether definitions are shared, and thus where the boundary between governance and management is drawn? Stuart MacClure, writing in *The Times* (13 February 1992: 7), points to the basis of the problem:

The definition of the head's responsibilities vis-a-vis the governors are [*sic*] undoubtedly vague. The governors are charged
with 'the conduct of the school' which parliament has decided
should be under their 'direction'; but the same Education Act
makes clear that the 'determination and organization of the
secular curriculum' rests with the Head. Nobody knows exactly
where the dividing line runs.

One could take the position that this dividing line has to be worked
out in practice; that it comes down to cases, to the strength and
weakness of heads and governors, as Mr Green suggests. But uncertainty, trials of strength, manipulation and conflict (although
real and ever-present) hardly seem the basis for new flexibility or
clear and effective school leadership. We may perhaps no longer be
asking whether the head is a good leader, but whether he or she
is the leader at all. Evetts (1993: 64), reporting on interviews with
school heads, found that 'the contexts for negotiation were increased,
widened and made less predictable . . . The new budgetary constraints
as well as the moods of particular governing bodies were ill-defined
and in any case were liable to change.' Let us pursue this a little further via some comments from Mrs Silver, headteacher of Overbury
Comprehensive, which take up Mr Green's concerns.

> I think there are some very articulate governors, very involved
> as to what is going on, and they run the risk of interfering in
> management, as opposed to setting policy . . . I mean the gov-
> ernors are always supportive of the school and a lot of them
> like to come to the school, not to direct what's going on, thank
> goodness, yet, but just to find out what's going on, almost in
> terms of sort of governors' inspecting . . . But my parent gov-
> ernors in particular, a couple of them found it very difficult to
> understand the difference between governing and managing,
> and do want to be involved far more than they are or as I see
> as being appropriate at the moment. Its all quite difficult enough
> with staff trying to get the line between leadership and consensus
> without actually then having to take [the same issues] to the
> governors. I sometimes spend hours presenting a paper so that
> they can actually tell me what to do . . . They want to feel as
> though they have got power, well let's face it they have got
> power, and they want to be exercising that power. I find gov-
> ernors' meetings increasingly uncomfortable . . . As if I haven't

got enough to do without managing the governors as well, or feeling that I need to, in order to take the school in the direction that I feel it needs to go.

Mrs Silver's last comment seems to capture the basic contradiction in the current UK version of school-centred leadership: the meaning of leadership is caught between autonomy and responsibility on the one hand and accountability and 'community' participation on the other. And this contradiction is deeply rooted in the politics of the reform process. Again, on the one hand, the headteacher is a key figure in the process of reform. But, on the other, the Conservative government is deeply suspicious of professional expertise in any area of public service.

At least three, rough and ready, discourses remain in play in the field of uncertainties which surround school governance. The 'professional' discourse of headship is one. This is informed and invested by images of headteacherly authority which stretch back to the reform of the public schools in the nineteenth century; as well as, in some cases, a new managerial professionalism transplanted from commercial settings and fostered by training courses and proselytizing texts. Another is the business or entrepreneurial discourse, often informed and invested by the business experience and perspectives of school governors (this separation out of big business managerialism and small business entrepreneurialism has not been much attended to in the consideration of school management and needs further careful teasing out – but I shall not attempt to do that here). The last is the empowerment of community discourse. This is articulated by a few governors in a few schools but takes on a variety of forms ranging from versions of accountability on the one hand, to versions of partnership or community representation on the other. And this third is certainly least well represented with the contemporary politics of education. It fits uneasily with the disaggregated, 'consumer' perspective which predominates in education policy texts. The chair of Governors at Northwark Park School explains:

And then there's the issue of policy which I think it'll take us decades, rather than years, to evolve. The policy changes of the school ought not to be all that frequent, as they are at the moment, and I think that's a bit confusing. But you would expect there to be a genuine partnership, if you like, between community, parent community and professionals so that you

arrive at a understandable proposition of what you are going to
try to do and why you're going to try to do it, and I think that's
the most underweighted part at the moment, because there is
no history. I can remember when the adventurous idea of parent
governors was introduced by the ILEA, so that must be in the
sixties or seventies, but it's quite recent that parental involvement in schools. Certainly when I first became active, it was
almost disapproved that you should have governors who knew
anything at all about what the school did, and so on.

This can be set directly against the comments of the headteacher
of Trumpton School, articulated from within the 'professional' discourse. This is indicative of the nascent antagonism between the
professional and the community.

Yes, and they know that full well, and they do work which is
appropriate for them to do, I mean they don't come here and
lean over my shoulder every day, which would be most inappro-
priate, and whilst I never ever say anything in explicit terms
with them, I get them to understand what it is they're supposed
to do.

I literally do use them quite substantially and get them very
busy and organized into doing the sorts of things that are proper
for governors to do, which leaves them far less time to come
and do other things, which is fair enough. I think . . . I'm not
pushy with them, and I will not interfere with the ways things
are going with them unless they're getting off the path. Then
I ease them in again, sort of gently, and eventually they get to
where I think they should have been in the first place, which
is fair enough, and because I don't push them too hard, they've
got quite a lot of faith, I think. So I get most of the things
devolved to me that in some schools are not. So, for example,
I have full financial power, they have not, there is no limita-
tion, whereas some schools have said, over such and such the
chair of the governors must be asked, I don't have that.

There is an underlying awareness evident on both sides that there
is the potential for conflict here. There is a terrain of uncertainty to
be negotiated. The locus of control is ill-defined. Thomas (1992:
332), makes the point that 'a governing body may become a proper
decision-making forum only if the Head is prepared to *sponsor* that
development'. The chair of governors at Northwark Park again:

I think we have a good head and the school has a bright future, but certainly not a head who is used to bringing her ideas up to a governing body who could say no, and I think that is the problem. That the head assumes she assumes that when she is satisfied, the governors will agree, which they usually do. And she believes, I suspect, that it is the teachers who run the school, it is. And that she is a teacher, and you will find in talking to her, I mean you may not feel this, but certainly I feel that she regards herself as a pedagogue, and there is a school of thought that you should leave the teachers to run the schools, and that external intervention is not welcomed. And she's not strident and not aggressive with it, and I think that she has a good relationship with her governing body, but I think that her basic philosophy is that the governors ought to keep out of most of the important decisions about education.

There are issues of both power and culture embedded in these tensions. And behind both there is the complex and heavy weight of the contested history of post-war welfare policy and ideology in the UK. That is to say, different political conceptions of the role of education and educational politics underlie the discourses and the struggles, however subtle, currently enjoined around the governance of schools. The 'professional' discourse is rooted in a history of public sector/welfare state paternalism. This trades upon the maintenance of a high level of practitioner autonomy and limited citizen/consumer participation in policy or decision making. It was developed through a period of minimal strategic uncertainty. In Ferris's (1985) terms, this discourse addressed 'collective distribution claims' (via comprehensive education) but embodied a 'failure of moral vision'. It never achieved a basis of strongly shared values or mutual dependency. The 'business' discourse is a counter-discourse, which is articulated through neo-liberal economics and New Right politics (see Chapters 4 and 5) and asserts a financial management/effectiveness perspective, as well as a small business mentality – the entrepreneur in the competitive market place. A parent governor, an architect, points up this position and its difficult relationship to 'professionalism':

Sometimes there's a sort of . . . because I think the senior management team don't see themselves as business, they are teachers. That's the prime aim, is to actually teach children, and they're not here to take in a product and churn it out at the

other end. They're dealing with people, and I sometimes think
they feel a little upset by the fact that the governors sometimes
do look upon it as a business and you've got to sort of reconcile
that. We've got to come to terms with that and find a mid-line,
where the governors are satisfied, particularly those with
financial experience, are satisfied that yes, the school is not
going to make a loss, yes, it is doing the right things to attract
pupils, and it is spending its money wisely.

The empowerment discourse is also a counter-discourse. It stands
in antagonistic relationship to both of the others but is represented
primarily in rhetoric rather than in widespread practice (Vincent
1993). Its historical status in the post-war UK politics of education is
one of irritant and unrealized hope. Woods (1992), however, sees
the possibility of realizing a hybrid version of business and community discourses which would interpolate the 'consumer-citizen'. I am
less sanguine and see real and irreconcilable differences between a
consumption orientation and the commodification of education, and
democratic participation in school decision making; between collective, community decision making and privatized, self-interested
decision making (see Chapter 8; I will return to teacher–parent
relations below). Thomas (1992: 333) points up another paradox
embedded in all this: 'It is an irony of a reform which places such
emphasis upon individual self-interest that much of its successful
management may well depend upon governors being altruistic and
headteachers being committed to values which cherish community
participation in social institutions.'
    Two further points about headteacher–governor relationships since
1988. First, given the new 'powers' of governors, the working relationship between the headteacher and chair of governors is crucial
in the achievement and maintenance of a line of demarcation between
governance and management. The specificity of this relationship is
a key point of focus for future research. Second, the constitution of
governing bodies varies significantly from school to school, not least
in terms of the social class and occupational positions of governors.
The variations in their habitus and cultural capital mean that different skills, values, concerns and levels of articulacy are brought into
play. These can constitute valuable resources to the school (e.g. free
legal, business and architectural advice) and/or threaten the
managerial prerogative of the school's management team. Thus,

Deem (1992: 12) argues, 'who becomes empowered and what they do with those powers is more crucial than an abstract notion of empowerment regarded as a "good thing" in itself.' Deem is also careful to stress that governors differ from one another in their stance towards education and their definition of their task and role, and that these cannot be simply read off from categorical identities or class position. She also makes a useful and important distinction between 'collective interest' and 'consumer interest' governors.

Leadership, colleagueship and management

The second aspect of change relationships relating to 'new headship', the relationships of heads with their teaching staff, also raises questions about what leadership means. There are two aspects to this. First, heads are now *de facto* (through the governing body) the employers of teachers. The possibilities of colleagueship are constrained by this. Second, the effective reconstruction of the head's role, as budget manager, entrepreneur and promoter of the school, diverts the values, purposes and concerns of the head from matters educational to matters financial and managerial. Thus, not only are the priorities of managers and teachers diverging but there is a clear-cut separation emerging between policy concerns, vested in management, and a more limited role of execution, for the teachers (see Bowe and Ball with Gold 1992, and Chapter 4). Evetts (1993: 63), drawing on an interview study of school heads, suggests an increase in 'the likelihood of conflict arising in schools over staffing matters ... Heads' attempts to maintain consensus in their schools over staffing would be increasingly clouded by their negotiating skills in micropolitical bargaining with staff and governors.'

The gap between head and teachers is ramified by the recent policies of the UK government on teachers' salaries. The salary gap between heads and teachers has been carefully and deliberately widened both by higher pay awards nationally for heads and by the introduction of institutional increases. And, significantly given the previous discussion, the negotiation of institution salary increases and pay supplements related to performance for heads now takes place between individual heads and their governors. *The Times Education Supplement* (22 March 1991: 6) reported that: 'Scores of headteachers are jeopardizing good relations with their teachers by negotiating salary top ups for themselves.' And Dr Alan Leech, headteacher of Bohunt Community School in Hampshire and chair-person of the NUT's education and equal opportunities committee, was quoted as saying that: 'My view is that any head would be unwise to seek to undertake individual negotiations irrespective of the pay policy for the rest of the employees. The consequence of that is distress, dismay and unhappiness with a degree of demoralization with the rest of the teaching force.' But in more general terms, we should see these changes in pay and conditions for heads as part of the construction of managers' self-interest and a new culture of man-agement. Part of this is a changed structure of accountability; that is, the headteacher is now primarily accountable to governors rather than to staff.

Again, the point is that the possibilities of 'new headship' are framed and constrained by policy decisions which affect and reorient the head/teacher relationship. Leader/follower relationships do not develop outside these structural changes. While heads may now have more sources of potential influence and effect in relation to teachers and their work, the teachers' commitment to overall institutional achievement may be reduced rather than enhanced. Estrangement seems more common than collaboration. Empowering heads is very different from empowering schools. Rather, we are seeing the emergence of a line management culture within schools. One Flightpath teacher explained that

> We're into a situation now where I think we definitely are not in control, I don't feel in control. I may feel consulted, but the consultations are more or less about what's been discussed and decided, as opposed to what in fact we are going to do . . . even heads of department are becoming like that too, they're finding their room for manoeuvre is not that great either . . . they're being told to implement things, therefore they're coming over as being, not perhaps as dictatorial, that's too harsh a phrase, but perhaps as being determinedly persuasive . . . And no doubt they're looking over their shoulder, because they're being told, look, you are the one that's accountable, so get these things done.

One interpretation of all this is to see the new pay arrangements for heads, the rhetoric of headteacher flexibility and the support and legitimation given for the insertion of management principles into schools as part of a strategy of political cooptation of heads by government. David Hart, General Secretary of the National Associa- tion of Headteachers, certainly hinted at something of this in inter- view. 'The Secretary of State certainly needs heads. They are the lynchpins of the system, and he can't deliver the reforms without the heads. And he has to recognise that in pay terms soon, and in terms of our negotiating rights and conditions of service' (quoted in Ball 1990b: 67). And he did!

I am not suggesting here that all individual heads subscribe to or succumb to the temptations of cooptation, but rather that the pres- sures and conditions of their work in these circumstances make certain leadership roles less easily obtainable and more risky than others. The gap between headteacher/managers and teachers, in terms of both values and relationships, is exacerbated by the overall change in role orientation by headteachers. Their work perspective is in- creasingly dominated and contained by financial and administrative concerns. Less and less time is left for educational leadership.

> I mean I've just fixed a deal for the maintenance of the site. I've got a new schedule, which has 3000 more items on it than the one that the LEA were using and it's cheaper than the LEA's. Now that's a damn good deal. So yes, there's all sorts of things that you can do, and you'd be amazed at how know- ledgeable I am about drains, plumbing, electricity. The disturb- ing aspect of that is what it does do is prevents me from doing the things that I think are really terribly important as a head. Which is perambulating around the classrooms at least once every day, looking at pupils' work and so on, which I used to do before.
>
> (Head of Trumpton)

Headteachers and teachers are differently positioned in all this in relation to key environmental issues and potentially in relation to key values in the organization. And again these nascent tensions carry with them the possibility of micropolitical conflict and demoral- ization in the organization (Ball 1987).

> It's not just marketing, it's part of the ethos of the whole school, the public or community view of the school that the head and deputies get very much involved in. People feel that they are not addressing the needs of the school. Because they feel that their perception of the needs of the school are different from

the perception of deputy heads. And there becomes a void
between what management want and what classroom teachers
want and I think that's a dangerous situation, a very dangerous
situation. And I don't think it's the fault of management, I
think it's the fault of the system.

                                   (Teacher governor, Trumpton School)

The struggle over values is also a struggle over language, culture
and self-perceptions (see Chapter 8). Again this struggle is informed
by the histories and discourses discussed above. The micropolitics
of the organization represents and replays a larger-scale scenario of
educational politics. The head of Parsons School explains the terrain
of struggle.

I think it still is the province of the most senior managers in
the school principally, but it's increasingly being used throughout the school. The culture is changing. But I also think that
all levels are aware that it's not just about money, it's about
'management', and everybody is a manager, everybody has
resources to manage. So the culture is changing, the language
is changing, and we are using the language of the marketplace
more and more . . . you hear people talking about cornering
the market in this particular aspect of school work or where
is our market, who are our customers, our clients? Some object
very strongly and feel that this is not the way in which they as
professionals think teachers should be operating. But that tends
to be the old, rather patronizing left attitude, which is gradually
growing out. There are far fewer people now expressing that
perspective.

Parents, markets and institutional response

The third aspect of relational change brought about by the 1988 Act
is that between heads and parents. As chief executive of Downtown
Comprehensive plc the headteacher now confronts the parent as a
customer and consumer. Each child through the school gate is worth
a fixed amount to the school in income. In oversubscribed schools
this may have little impact on the relationship between the head and
any individual parent: the Head controls access to a desirable commodity and exclusivity and exclusion may actually enhance the institution's attractiveness to consumers (see Chapter 7). But it is clear

that in general terms attentiveness to the consumer has heightened
significantly in the new market conditions. Here again the diver-
gence between a market and an educational orientation is in evidence. The head is caught between financial judgements which are
oriented to keeping customers satisfied and the professional judgements of teaching staff oriented to good practice and, in some settings, social justice. The implications of this tension for the head's
role as educational leader are clear. Let us take a specific example
from Flightpath Comprehensive. The senior deputy head, Mr Gray,
explains:

> we had an interesting meeting recently in which I was at the
> parent–teachers association, which generally is a fairly tame
> sort of thing, and then out of the blue somebody asked me a
> question unrelated to anything I was prepared to talk about
> that evening, about whether anybody was doing mixed-ability
> teaching under these new arrangements. And I happen to know
> that the English department decided to do mixed-ability
> teaching in the lower school, and so I said yes, the English
> department, and if I'd have said that they were considering
> child abuse, I probably wouldn't have had such a violent reaction
> as I got from that group of about 30 or 40 parents who attended
> that meeting. Unprepared for all this I said, 'Look folks, I didn't
> actually make this particular decision. I do back it, support it,
> but if you really want to know more, you ought to meet the
> English department and talk about it.' So we've set up a meeting
> on Monday, which has all the makings of a first-rate row, because
> parents have marshalled themselves for the first time on any
> issue, apart from the building development which they've been
> very stroppy about one way or another, on this whole question
> of mixed-ability in English. They've written to every parent and
> they've said, 'do you really want mixed ability in English?' and
> the English department feel as though there is some massive
> plot against them.

Parental questioning of teaching approaches has a history that
certainly predates the 1988 Act, and although it appears to be a new
phenomenon at this school it would be wrong to assume a wave of
'parent power' generated by the ERA. The general changes are more
subtle than that. None the less, the beginnings of a change in institutional culture and in school–parent relations in the new operating

context of the market do reflect a new inflection to parental 'involvement'. In this case a public meeting was arranged, where the
English teachers and the LEA English advisor were required to put
their case for mixed-ability and attempt to convince the sceptical
parents. One of the other deputies made it clear that his criterion
for deciding on the future of mixed-ability in English was the
presentation of a 'convincing argument' to parents.

> There are two things that can happen at that meeting, either
> English will convince the parents that within mixed-ability they
> can push every individual, which would be great. My personal
> convictions are not for mixed-ability. I've seen some good
> teachers teach it very well, but the average teacher struggles to
> cater for it. But I come from a maths/science background. So
> excepting my personal bias I am quite prepared, if they put a
> convincing argument for it, then fair enough, and convince the
> parents, that's my criterion.

There is a tension here between the traditional teacher professionalism and the forces of the market as criteria for educational decision making, a tension that senior staff were only too aware of.

> I must admit I am in a divided situation here, because I do
> believe very fundamentally that teachers should have the right
> to decide the best way of organizing something to achieve the
> aims you've set them. On the other hand, I do believe that we
> are serving a public. Now if a public, who now have four gov-
> ernors, whereas the teachers only have two, if the public don't
> see eye-to-eye with the teachers on something you have the
> makings of a really big row, because both people have high
> expectations of success. The teachers expect their professional-
> ism to be acknowledged and the parents quite simply take their
> kids away. They're now in the position to send their kids to a
> school which suits the way they're organized. Now our local
> schools: Hamfield go in for quite a bit of streaming; Langdale,
> who've previously not been massive rivals for us because they
> haven't got it together in academic terms, they are now market-
> ing themselves much more and are talking about top ability
> sets and so on. And quite honestly if the English department
> don't give a good account of themselves to the parents, then
> I'm afraid we will get people withdrawn.
>
>   (Senior deputy)

Despite the example above from Flightpath, it would be incorrect to suggest that large numbers of parents have taken up significantly changed roles in relations with schools as a result of the 1988 Act and The Parents' Charter. Few teachers perceive major change, although there are some differences between schools which seem related to the social composition of the parent body.

> According to the government certainly there's all these parents just sitting there saying, 'Oh, let us have power in our schools, we can't wait.' I have to tell you they aren't, they don't want to know, they want to sit inside round their fire in the winter and watch television and go out and enjoy their gardens in the summer. They do not want to come here and run this school. They want you to educate their kids, they trust you to do it, presuming they've given you the trust, and as I say apart from individuals in trouble. It works well enough. They come to things connected with their own individual children.
>
> (Head of Trumpton)

What has changed, as indicated already, is the *attentiveness* of schools and headteachers to their clientele (attentiveness is different to responsiveness). In effect, headteachers are now more alert to the 'market signals', to perceptions of and particularly discontents about their school. And they are more likely to be *responsive* when it seems relevant or expedient to do so. This again sets in a nascent tension: between responsiveness and judgement, or responsiveness and value commitments (this is explored more fully in Chapter 8). The head of Fletcher School illustrates both attentiveness and the precarious balance between responsiveness and commitment.

> We are a comprehensive school, we're committed to the comprehensive ideology or system or organization, and we do it very well. I mean, take your pick, see what we do, what we offer the children, what we provide for children, what they achieve, the atmosphere of the school. And that basically has remained the same, so I don't see that we have made any fundamental alteration. I think we've become more sensitive to and aware of the need to make sure that we've got our finger on the pulse, so to speak, so that we do know what's going on around us, what is happening in other authorities, and it's made us very conscious of the need to continue to attract parents, but I mean that has always been the case.

The balance sometimes may appear to be dependent rather than assertive; instrumental rather than principled.

> I'm confident that our values and what we stand for as a school are those which will attract parents to send their children here, and if we were pedalling something that parents weren't interested in, then clearly we'd need to look at the whole thing again, but I don't think that is the case, and I think the evidence proves that to be the case, we have attracted a lot of parents to send their children here.

And it may, in practice, be unclear how many compromises and accommodations can be admitted with the integrity of a vision or commitment remaining intact. The tensions evident here are generic: the professional/public service and market budgetary perspectives of 'new headship' are not easily reconciled. The head of Parsons sees a significant shift of positions across these tensions as already having taken place.

> We now see ourselves increasingly as delivering a service that parents want. There has been a shift from the previous position which was: this is our school, this is our philosophy, and it would not be the parents articulating the philosophy it would be the professional articulating the philosophy. This is what we stand for, these are our values, this is the way we interpret our value system, put it into practice, therefore this is what your child will experience at our school. There is now increasingly: what do you want from us? How can we provide it? So we are much more conscious that parents are entitled to demand the service that they want. But it's not the child, it's the parent. Now, I have all sorts of questions in my mind about whether that's right, but I think that that shift has taken place.

Thus, both the balance and axis of control over schooling are changing here: from teacher to parent, and from student to parent. This fits within what Brown (1990) calls the 'third wave' of education reform and the 'ideology of parentocracy'.

Conclusion

In all this the locus and meaning of school leadership seems to be blurred, to say the least. Rather than representing a new organizational paradigm, the 'new headship' is constructed by a set of powerful contradictions. And these contradictions are embedded in long-standing public and political discourses. Rather than offering a resolution or clarification, the current policies for school governance are a reorientation and obfuscation. They reorient the 'economy of power' within schools but misrepresent autonomy and authority. The policies which currently inform headship in the UK seem to have created a framework for impossibility, which schools and headteachers are left to deal with. But the headteacher must continue to inhabit a set of pointed and potentially conflictual relationships with governors, staff and parents, which would appear to have narrowed down the space available for developmental or democratic interpretations of educative leadership.

The role of governors is equally an obfuscation rather than a matter of real change. The new responsibilities of governors and the election of parent representatives allow the state to argue that, together with choice, there is a significant degree of parent empowerment and an increase in their influence over school policies. In practice, change is superficial. Parental governors are typically recruited rather than elected. Their relationship to the main body of parents is vague and distant. And most governors lack the time, information and will to take their apparent responsibilities seriously. Headteachers work hard to ensure that this is the way that things stay. Governance is thereby rendered into a ritualistic and symbolic but potentially unstable process. As far as headship is concerned, it is the change in relationships and in culture that is most significant in redefining heads' role and self-conception.

7

Education markets, choice and social class: the market as a class strategy in the UK and the USA[1]

This chapter sets out to clear away some of the theoretical under-growth which surrounds the market alternative in education and to establish a sociological agenda for researching and theorizing the education market. More specifically, it poses some questions about the effects of market forces on schools and on parents and about the benefits of the market for parents. It is about both the ideology and the practicalities of the education market.

The market, as a policy alternative to 'public monopoly education', is clearly education policy flavour of the decade across the western world. It is in danger of becoming unassailable. There is now in educational policy a well established, powerful and complex ideology of the market and a linked culture of choice which are underpinned by dangerous idealizations about the workings of markets, and the effects of parental choice and of 'profit' incentives in education.

One aspect of the development and survival of this ideology has been the careful and skilful avoidance by the organic intellectuals of the market, of any kind of reflexive critique. This avoidance involves: (a) their failure to apply the criticisms and assumptions made of and applied to 'public monopoly education', to market or choice-driven systems of education; (b) their use of idealizations of commodity markets when extolling the possibilities and benefits of market forces in education; (c) their failure to develop a grounded analysis of the particular conditions of a market in educational services; (d) their failure to explore fully the real and potential inequities arising within an education market, even when these are pointed up in their own theoretical work; (e) their failure to carry over assumptions about rational self-interest from their critique of 'monopoly public professionals' into their idealizations of 'educational entrepreneurs'. In other words, their characterizations of public professionals paint a bleak picture of 'self-interested' behaviour and give little attention to the commitment to 'service', whereas their characterizations of the 'educational entrepreneur' take self-interested behaviour to be a necessary virtue.

What I want to do is to take seriously some of the criticisms of 'public monopoly education' and apply them to market or choice-driven systems, and, so far as I am able, to begin to construct a model of the education market. I will draw upon some tit-bits of research evidence for this and highlight some specific elements of current US practice and UK government education policy. And I will finish with a stark conclusion. That is, the implementation of market reforms in education is essentially a class strategy which has as one of its major effects the reproduction of relative social class (and ethnic) advantages and disadvantages. I am not arguing that these consequences are intended by the advocates of the market but neither should they be regarded as entirely unexpected given the values and processes of the market. In order to understand the way the market operates as a strategy of class advantage, the interplay of three key elements has to be grasped: the self-interest of some producers; the self-interest of some consumers; and the control of the performance criteria of market organizations, which in the UK lies with the state.

The case against 'public monopoly education'

The case against the 'public monopoly' school is simple and powerful and I will not rehearse it at great length. (a) The financial support (via taxation) for and continuance of the monopoly school is not linked directly to the satisfaction of clients. (b) The absence of profit or loss motives for school managers leads to conservative, self-serving, minimalist, survival strategies (Morrell 1989: 25). (c) The decision-making of these schools is dominated by self-interest: 'The current procedures for resource allocation at the building level have more to do with the equitability of adult working conditions than with the production of responsive learning environments for children' (Mann 1981). (d) State monopoly schooling generates an inefficient and stultifying bureaucracy which encourages waste and inhibits responsiveness to parental concerns. (e) All the foregoing 'conspire' to depress standards and inhibit the press for excellence (however, the last three of the above rest upon a rather underdeveloped social psychology of organisation and motivation). (f) The 'sameness' of monopoly schools, together with restrictions on enrolment, removes the possibility of choice for parents and the possibility of ensuring that their child's needs are best met (I would suggest that this sameness is radically overemphasised; see Ball *et al.* forthcoming). (g) Chubb and Moe (1990) add a further dimension to this critique: that the democratic control of monopoly schools involves an imposition of the policies of dominant interest groups and office-holders on the community as a whole, thus creating a system of 'winners' and 'losers'; and 'The "losers" have the obligation to accept and help finance these policies and structures, however much they may be opposed to them' (p. 28). And related to this, (h) within a system of democratic control 'parents and students are not well enough organised to be very powerful. In the struggle to control public authority, they tend to be far outweighed by teachers' unions, professional organisations, and other entrenched interests' (Chubb and Moe 1990: 31). This critique and its implications provide the basis for the school related provisions of the UK government's 1988 Education Reform Act and are taken even further 1993 Education Act.

The case for markets and choice

To a great extent the case for the market is the simple converse of the above. Chubb and Moe, for example, make three key points about the education market, using as their model the private school sector in the USA: (a) that the owners of private schools have a strong incentive to please students and parents (it is taken for granted here that the same things will please both), thus making the schools responsive; (b) that switching between schools will move students and resources from the unpopular/unresponsive schools to the popular/responsive ones; (c) that this provides a mechanism of natural selection through which unpopular schools are bound to be forced to close or change themselves. In some ways Chubb and Moe are more up front about the down-side of the Darwinian metaphor than many market advocates. There is a tendency (another idealization) by politicians in particular to talk about markets only in terms of positive effects and outcomes: they envision a market utopia where every school gets better (irrespective of resource differences) and the magic of competition ensures that every consumer is happy – Adam Smith meets Walt Disney.

> The evidence is striking and abundant. Almost without exception, wherever choice has been attempted – Minnesota, East Harlem, San Francisco, Los Angeles, and a hundred other places in between – choice has worked . . . Bad schools get better. Good ones get better still, and entire schools systems have been restored to public confidence by the implementation of these choice plans. Disaffected families have been brought from private schools back into public education. Any school reform that can boast such success deserves our attention, our emphasis, and our effort.
>
> (President George Bush, quoted in Paulu 1989: 25–6)

The National Governors Association shares the same naive, idealistic enthusiasm.

> If we first implement choice, true choice among public schools, we unlock the values of competition in the market place. Schools that compete for students, teachers, and dollars will, by virtue of the environment, make those changes that will allow them to succeed.
>
> (National Governors Association Time for Results 1986, quoted in Paulu 1989: 14)

Some politicians are less dewy-eyed, though. Keith Joseph, UK Secretary of State for Education from 1981 to 1986 and neo-liberal guru to Margaret Thatcher, explained his commitment to choice thus:

> I think that national agencies tend to be producer lobbies, like nationalised industries. One of the main virtues of privatisation is to introduce the idea of bankruptcy, the potential of bankruptcy. That's why I like opting out . . . of course I wanted vouchers. Simply because you transfer in one go from the producers to the consumers . . . I don't claim that all consumers are wise, of course not, but some will be able to exercise choice which they can't exercise now. [Some again.]
>
> (Interview with Keith Joseph, quoted in Ball 1990b: 63)

It also seems clear that the Conservative government in the UK sees the market in education as a way of reducing the significant level of spare capacity in the school system – by allowing choice to target unpopular schools for closure.

> Ministers would say that it remains the case that there is a quite large surplus of school accommodation, still throughout the country . . . and the authorities have not yet fully realised the potential for taking places out of use, and Ministers would say that as parental views, as expressed through choice of school, help authorities to take hard decisions, then painful though it may be, that can actually be beneficial.
>
> (Interview with DES civil servant, quoted in Ball 1990b: 66)

In the UK, the neo-liberal, Hayekian vision of the market, to which Margaret Thatcher was converted in the mid-1970s, underpinned both the small business, self-employment revolution in the UK economy in the mid-1980s and the market reforms being implemented in the education system and National Health Service. It is again a utopian vision of a perfect market made up of numerous small providers, and the competition of all against all: consumer heaven. The reality of the small business revolution is, however, not so heavenly. In the last quarter of 1991 there were five and a half thousand commercial bankruptcies in the UK, that is one in forty of all businesses, a rise of 40 per cent on the same period in 1990 (British Chambers of Commerce 7 February 1992). The market is cruel!

It is also important to set alongside this economics-based rationale for reform the elements of its attendant political vision. Margaret Thatcher's economics closely relate to her very individualistic conception of democracy. This is very much what Barber (1984: 25) would call 'thin democracy': 'Oblivious to that essential human interdependency that underlies all political life.' Or what Gutmann (1987: 28) calls 'a state of families', which places 'educational [and all other social authority] exclusively in the hands of parents, thereby permitting parents to choose a way of life consistent with their familial heritage.' Both aspects are captured in her oft quoted remark that 'There is no such thing as society, only individuals and families.' Morrell (1989: 17) suggests that this remark 'is an expression of the Hayekian view in epigrammatic form'. And she also notes that 'Hayek is particularly concerned to argue against the involvement of

Government in the life of the citizen', and goes on to say that 'Hayek and Friedman were in reality the co-godparents of Kenneth Baker's [1988] Education Act' (Morrell 1989: 26). A second, and closely related, element is the elimination or reduction in influence of intermediate democratic institutions, particularly local government and, within local government, local education authorities. Those agencies which are seen as distorting or inhibiting market relations are being removed. What is being worked towards is a consumer rather than a citizenship democracy: the former resting upon 'self interest registered privately and with uncertain (though often malign) public consequences'; the latter involving 'a concern for the well-being of others as well as the health of society' (Ranson 1990: 15).

Self-interest and choice

Overall in the policy literature on social markets, particularly the education market, the emphasis is upon the demand side, on choice. Less overall is said about the behaviour of producers in the market, apart from rather abstract notions about incentive and entrepreneurship. What get glossed over are the mechanisms of institutional survival in the market – most crucially competition. While the structures and processes and dynamics of business and commodity markets are supposed to work their magic on educational institutions and are readily talked about, the *values* of business and competition are not. It is again idealistically assumed that educational values will remain unblemished by the demands of responsiveness and survival – evidence suggests that in reality they do not (see Ball 1990c and Chapters 5 and 8). It is neither clear nor logical that the changes produced by market reforms will be education led. Rather it follows that they will be financially led and will rest upon the self-interest of the institutional employees, who want to ensure the future of their jobs or to achieve greater rewards (Boyd 1982: 114). This base reality is not directly addressed in either public choice or market theories. Rather, both concentrate on the iniquities of public organizations, in which 'a kind of reciprocity with employees and key interest groups is created that, along with the executive's self-interest, tends to foster the maximisation of budgets rather than profits (i.e. consumer or client satisfaction)' (Boyd 1982: 115). It seems to be assumed that altruism is subordinate to self-interest in the monopoly school but that self-interest is subordinate to altruism in the market school. The

values and ethics of the two systems logically indicate quite the re-
verse. There is every possibility of a new form of loose-coupling: the
disconnection of financial management and income maximization
from the production technology of education. And if, as seems
evident (Bowe and Ball with Gold 1992), principals become *primarily*
concerned with financial management and public relations within
the education market place, then the *educational leadership*, which
researchers find to be so strongly associated with effective schooling,
will be minimal, if not totally compromised (see Chapter 6).

Now public choice theorists (PCTs) and market theorists might
well argue that what they are suggesting is a change in the nature of
self-interest produced by the change in the incentive environment.
But this seems to have little support from work related to 'theories
of the firm'. Levacic (1991: 8) makes this point very clearly:

A firm, whatever its organisational form, is not run in the interests of its customers. This is only ensured by means of the
regulation provided by competitive product and capital markets, buttressed by legal safeguards. If these do not function
adequately to project customers' interests, then the firm can
earn monopoly profits for the benefit of the owners or instead
be run by the managers in their and the employees' interests
as reflected in higher costs.

It seems valid to presume that the self-interested, advantage-
maximizing individualism of consumers does apply equally to the
producers. We should thus expect: that they would seek to recruit
more able students, in order to make life easier for themselves and
ensure good performance outcomes (see Moore and Davenport 1990);
that they would turn away students with expensive learning needs in
order to maximize the impact of resources on outcomes; that they
would concentrate resources internally on those students with highest
ability and/or the most vocal and influential parents. Thus, the self-
interest of the educational entrepreneurs is linked to the self-interest
of those parents wanting and able to pursue relative advantage in the
education market. Moore and Davenport (1990: 201) found in a
study of 'choice' systems in four US cities that:

Given the discretion exercised in recruitment, screening, and
selection, there was an overwhelming bias toward establishing
procedures and standards at each step in the admissions process
that screened out 'problem' students and admitted the 'best'

students, with 'best' being defined as students with good academic records, good attendance, good behaviour, a mastery of English, and no special learning problems.

Marketeers' responses to such evidence, typically that greater regulation or different structures of incentives are needed, seem inevitably to lead to a position where the market always works best except when it does not. Basically, incentives in education and the social psychology of teaching are not fully grasped by marketeers.

There is a further difficulty embedded in the supply-side thinking of market theorists in education: that is, the resolution of autonomy (Chubb and Moe 1990: 37) with responsiveness. Autonomy is linked to arguments about specialization and efficiency. Responsiveness relates to notions about consumer sovereignty. If the market operates as a disciplinary system, in which there are 'strong forces at work – arising from the technical, administrative and consumer-satisfaction requirements of organizational success' (Chubb and Moe 1990: 37) – then to describe schools working inside this system as autonomous seems at best misleading. The whole conceptualization here remains under-theorized and under-researched (see also Chapter 5).

I have already noted the paradox in the UK of surplus places and oversubscribed schools. As the market does its theoretical work of natural selection, the less popular schools close and the surplus reduces then the pressure of competition for students also reduces, given the fixed number of students available at any point in time – this is inelastic demand. Without the pressure of surplus places the dubious social psychology of competition also ceases to work. Problems of oversubscription are likely to increase as new 'choices' are fed into the reduced system and it becomes easier for 'successful' organizations to defend their position via selection. Indeed, selection is, and will increasingly become, a 'selling point'; what you get is who you go with. Some schools in the UK are also manipulating their intakes by using the option of exclusion more readily, in order both to rid themselves of 'difficult' students and to demonstrate to potential clients that discipline and safety are taken very seriously ('Alarm over sharp rise in exclusions' (*Times Educational Supplement* 3 January 1992); 'Government told that LMS encourages schools to shut out difficult pupils: authorities want end to exclusion loophole' (*Times Educational Supplement* 10 February 1992)).

Excluded students have their 'choice' taken away from them and are hardly likely to be welcomed by other schools once their 'reputation' is known (ethnic minority students are disproportionately subject to such exclusions from schools in London; Bryant 1991). Here, unlike most other markets, *who* the client is matters: quality and reputation are related in good part to the clientele themselves, not solely to the service. What is being produced as a result is a stratified system made up of some schools which can afford to turn away certain clients and other schools that must take any they can get (Walford 1993). The situation of the teachers and managers in the former does not seem to differ significantly from that so roundly criticized by Hirschmann (1970) and others in public monopoly schooling: 'it spares them the "psychic costs" they would incur in dealing with these clients and enables them to enjoy the "best of all monopoly profits . . . a quiet life"' (Boyd 1982: 120). The market mechanism orients the public entrepreneur towards attracting the *effective consumer and the value-adding client*, and away from a concern with service towards a commitment to survival.

> The specific theories developed out of the public choice approach thus should be evaluated according to how well they predict or explain behaviour, not according to how well they correspond to humanistic notions of the complexity of humans and of social behaviour.
>
>   (Boyd 1982: 113–14)

A political market

Clearly, it is possible to write about market-based models of education in general terms; but the choice/market lobby is certainly a loose confederation (Cookson 1992) rather than a coherent single-minded voice. What I am trying to do here is to address what seem to be the shared touchstones of conceptualization and faith. But as well as theoretical diversity the relationships between theory and policy rhetoric and practice also play out differently in different settings. Certainly the ideological geography of market schooling is different in the UK and the USA.

The path the UK has hewn is far more radical in the undiluted application of ideologically driven policy. But in terms of either neoliberal economics or Choeism (the policy vision of Chubb and Moe) the UK education system is organized as a very strange market indeed. This serves to remind us that markets are neither natural nor neutral phenomena, they are socially and politically constructed. In the UK parents can, more or less, choose the school they want (as long as they do not live in rural areas and thus have access to only one school or cannot afford the transaction costs involved in choice), if there are places available (see below on the culture of choice), although as noted above there is considerable spare capacity in the system as a whole. Funding of schools then follows student numbers – 85 per cent of the local schools budget will soon be allocated on numbers alone. Thus, popular schools thrive and can normally afford the best qualified teachers and specialists from shortage subject areas. (Remember, though, that overall education budgets are limited and in decline in many areas – and the funding which is available is also being redistributed through per capita related formulae, so that more for some students means less for others.) Unpopular schools will lose income and will find it difficult to match the teacher skills and curriculum depth of their better off rivals.

So in these respects there is a real or mimic market. Parents can *express a choice* for the school they want for their child. (Even if they do not *get* that choice in competition with other parents. In public and academic discourse about the education market the important distinction between expressing a choice and choosing is frequently and conveniently glossed over. Advocates play fast and loose with the success verb.) But there is also a National Curriculum, with legal force, which every school must teach. Parents, in the state sector, cannot choose between different curricula. The government has also invented new types of school: CTCs, modelled on Magnet schools and part sponsored by industry, and grant-maintained schools, schools which 'opt out' of local authority control and which receive enhanced funding direct from government (not because they are popular but because they 'opt out'). In neither case is the nature or form of schooling offered as a specific response to parent demand. These schools are the product of government intervention. The market is thus heavily constrained and singularly constructed by government. It is based on what Hayek (1980: 111) terms 'ordered competition' – a form of competition that is intended to achieve *particular* social and economic goals. Furthermore, the performance indicators of schooling are set by the government through a system of National Testing and the requirements of the Parents' Charter (1991). Is this

'real' choice? Is this a market? It certainly has the effect of a market
in creating competition between schools, but the possibilities of invention, entrepreneurship and expressions of minority interests or
commitments among parents are severely limited by political control
of the market.

In understanding the construction and workings of the political
market we also need to attend, in particular, to the control exerted
by the state over the indicators of performance – the information system that is supposed to provide the basis of choice. The importance
of this is highlighted by recent debates in the UK about the reporting
of school and teacher performance for public consumption. The UK
government remains committed to a raw score approach rather than
a valued added one, despite criticism from the government's own
local government watchdog agency, the National Audit Commission.
A raw score policy serves to reinforce selection of students by ability
in oversubscribed schools and subordinates the raising of education
standards to the reproduction of *relative advantage* in relation to other
market exchanges – i.e. the labour market. Here the 'best' schools
are not those which achieve most in terms of student learning but
those which are able to sift and select their intake most rigorously.
Hence it is of vital importance who controls the indicators, for what
purpose indicators are used and whose interests the indicators serve.
In the UK we might ask: if raising standards is a primary aim of
reform why are raw scores being used to compare schools? This
contradiction is not confined to the education market. In the development of a quasi-market within the health service attention has
been given to the ways in which the selection of patients, what is
called 'cream-skimming', and the exclusion of patients, 'silt-shifting',
can be minimized by building in financial disincentives. However,
Matsaganis and Glennerster (1993: 26) make the point that 'the
proposed DoH [Department of Health] formula [for fund-holding
general practitioners] *will* create incentives for cream-skimming'.

Questions about the effectiveness and appropriateness of indicators beg other questions about whether the indicators being required
of schools by government are what consumers most want to know
when making their choices. All the evidence in the UK from parental choice research indicates a distinct mismatch between the government's imposed indicators and the assumptions of market theorists,
and parents' actual preferences. Both those who 'chose' and the
factors which they advance in explanation of their choices appear at

variance with the assumptions and arguments which drive the erection of indicators. Adler *et al.* (1989: 134) conclude from their research that: 'the majority of parents who are exercising choice on behalf of their children seem to adopt a humanistic rather than a technological perspective'.

Now there is some danger of being mesmerized by fancy footwork here. Some market theorists argue that the intervention of the state means we do not have a 'real' market because market forces cannot have their full effect. Others, when taken to task about the possible excesses and opportunism of the market place, point to the regulatory role of the state in safeguarding consumer interests. From the perspective of policy analysis this may be a case of heads they win, tails you lose!

The ideology of the market

Now without going into too much detail let me lodge some concerns about some of the critiques and arguments underpinning the advocacy of the market which were sketched in above. Some of these concerns focus upon the arguments being mounted; others focus upon the conceptions of monopoly and market schooling that are deployed in these arguments. I will try to bring some evidence to bear upon these issues.

As noted earlier, there is a problem which runs through much of the advocacy writing on choice, which is that the market model is idealized and concomitantly the monopoly system is caricatured. On the one hand, Chubb and Moe (1990) make the point that democratic control of schools leads to a system of 'winners' and 'losers'; on the other hand there is a recognition that markets are imperfect, that 'The unequal distribution of income in society may bias certain markets in favour of the rich and against the poor' (p. 31) and that 'To the extent that these and other imperfections are serious, markets are less likely to generate the diversity, quality and levels of services that consumers want' (p. 32). These latter seem to be important points. They seem to be about 'winners' and 'losers' in the market place – something Chubb and Moe speak of as a fundamental flaw when discussing democratic politics. *It remains unclear as to why they are less important than the principle of choice and why we hear little more about them.* If, as some writers have argued, the public monopoly schools system has failed the children of the poor in particular, should

we not give particular consideration to the ways in which market
schooling also fails them? This is an argument which I try to address
in some detail below (see also Ball 1990c).

Why should it be *assumed* that all needs will be met in the market
place, or even that more needs will be met; that is ultimately an
empirical question. Public choice theorists regularly acknowledge
the inevitability of inequalities in the market (Tiebout 1956) but
seem to have little interest in pursuing the implications of these for
those who experience them. Clearly, as public choice theorists recognize, choice involves costs. For those for whom costs are pro-
hibitive there is no effective market in education. The market only
exists for some, and yet the PCTs and market politicians seem to have
little sociological interest in the others – the disenfranchised. The
exclusion of some from the possibilities of choice is taken to be
merely a technical glitch in the market utopia. Yet it is evident that
the inequality that is generated here ramifies with a set of other
consumption inequalities (housing, transport, recreation, etc.) which
are experienced by the same social groups (Boyd 1982: 119). The
'some' and the 'others' are the beneficiaries and victims of the market.
The systematic inattention to the plight of the losers in the market
suggests that market theories are underpinned and informed primarily by the values, interests and concerns of certain class groups and
fractions. Jonathan (1990: 19) adds a key point to this:

> Since education has exchange value as well as intrinsic value,
> and since its value-in-exchange, like that of any other currency,
> depends not on the amount of this good that an individual
> holds in absolute terms, but rather on the amount she holds
> *relative to others*, then a more favourable experience – in
> exchange value terms – secured for one child, entails a less
> favourable experience in those terms for some other child or
> children.

Chubb and Moe can be taken to task here in another way. In their
critique of democratic schooling they argue that 'The "losers" have
the obligation to accept and help finance these policies and structures however much they may be opposed to them' (p. 28). Yet the
creation of a market in educational services will surely produce a
similar outcome. The creation of an education market is a political
decision. Once it is established, both supporters and opponents of
the market will be subject to its vicissitudes and must contribute to

its running costs. Jonathan (1990: 20) argues that parents who find themselves thrust into an education market place,

> Being unable to affect the social situation of progressively less equal shares, but having the opportunity only to try and secure an advantageous share for those whose interests they hold in trust ... are under pressure to adopt a conservative and pru-dential social stance, thus contributing to cumulative social changes they have not directly chosen, and may very well not endorse.

Chubb and Moe's book is described as 'bristling with provocative policy implications' (Paul E. Peterson, book cover). Are we to assume that no one is or will be opposed to these policies or will object to helping to finance them? Chubb and Moe's defence to this point is likely to be one of their system achieving optimal efficiency – the greater good. But the question of value changes effected by market relations and the issue of inequalities are both displaced by such a response. And economics research provides little evidence of optimal efficiency being achieved empirically in other sorts of markets. Thus, what is indicated by this sleight of hand is not necessarily a sloppiness of argument (although it might be that also) but another aspect of unstated social psychology which underpins much market theory: The assumption of individual rational self-interest as a universal quality of human nature (see Jonathan 1990: 17). This is a further aspect of Barber's (1984) 'thin democracy', 'a politics that conceives of women and men at their worst' (p. 25). The constraints and demands of the market system will require those opposed to it to act as 'good' consumers to minimize disadvantage to their child.

Let me return to the issue of the imperfections of the market. One of the major conceptual problems arising from the application of market theory to the education system – apart from the tendency to idealize the market – is that we tend to get only one version of market theory, that version which trades upon the ideology of consumer sovereignty, as already noted.

This neo-classical vision of the market is notable for 'its methodological avoidance of issues concerning "power" or "political structure" in explaining economic institutions' (Gintis 1989: 66). The key aspect of this neglect, as far as schools are concerned, relates to Gintis's point that 'under competitive conditions, power in a capitalist economy accrues to agents on the short side of the market, i.e.

those whose trading partners are in a chronic state of excess supply'
(p. 69). Now, in many parts of the UK and many US cities there is
a surplus of schools places and by definition a fixed quantity of
school students. This excess of supply of places is what drives the
market and creates competition between institutions (although as
the 'unpopular' schools in the system close, the edge in the market
will be reduced). However, in both the UK and many US cities there
are some schools which are oversubscribed. They are in the position,
in one way or another, of choosing students, not the other way round.
They have power in the market and they can drive up the 'price' by
driving up entry requirements in terms of either measures of ability
or indicators of cultural capital. Recent newspaper coverage of the
issues of oversubscription and parental appeals points up both the
problematics of consumer sovereignty and the cultural demands of
consumer competition:

> Every parent's right to choose and lose
> > (*Independent* 18 July 1991)

> Community divided by fear and anger: thousands of parents
> denied first choice of schools for their child
> > (*Independent* 24 June 1991)

> Appeals soar over choice of school
> > (*Times Educational Supplement* 2 August 1991)

> Families find open market fails to deliver
> > (*Guardian* 22 July 1991)

> Any school as long as its not full
> > (*Independent* 18 July 1991)

Power here accrues to the producer. Insofar as this allows for
selection, as noted already, the energy and effort required to maintain superiority over other institutions in terms of raw performance
measures is reduced. There is little incentive for innovation or to
attend to the learning environment. Gintis (1989: 70) again makes
the point that 'it can be shown that "market tightening" (i.e., a
decline in equilibrium excess supply) entails higher firm rents and
lower product quality.' Even within a situation of excess supply it is
still doubtful whether it can be assumed that individual consumers are
empowered. In many cases, in the consumer goods market, the exchange between producer and consumer is not bilateral: 'an individual

consumer cannot affect the behaviour of producers' (Gintis 1989: 69). Here autonomy is high and responsiveness low, and assumptions about general improvements in system performance would seem to be misconceived.

Now it might be argued by market theorists that the 'success' of oversubscribed, self-interested schools will inevitably lead to emulation and competition for desirable students. Clearly, there is something in that, but this argument ignores the crucial role played by relative advantage in the educational market. For some consumers the point about choice is that they 'require' exclusivity and/or performance advantage – a levelling up of standards does not serve their interests. The sort of schooling they value is that sort which is difficult to get into and which produces superior performance outcomes. If all or many schools could offer the same service then the market system would have failed them, although total sameness is unlikely. But the market theorist might want to argue that the effects of competition would still be to raise the overall level of performance in the system and, perhaps, therefore to demand maximum effort from those schools determined to maintain their superior market theory position. But my point here is that the application of abstract market theory to education is based upon a partial and inadequate representation of the processes and effects of market forces in education and a partial and inadequate representation of the processes and effects of market forces in commodity markets.

Having established a terrain of concerns and debate related to the education market I want to develop the argument by looking at some evidence from those markets and systems of choice already operating in the USA and the UK.

Markets, choice and social inequality

Even in these early days of the education market there is evidence to suggest that the processes and effects of market forces are related to social class and ethnic differences in access to and distribution between schools. I want to suggest that in an education market (a) the strategic processes of choice systematically disadvantage working class families and (b) the link between choices and resources (via per capita funding) disadvantages working-class schools and communities (ramifying and interacting with other collective consumption inequalities). In others words, the operation and effects of an education market benefit certain class groups and fractions to the detriment and disadvantage of others. Again the market is not neutral. It presumes certain skills, competencies and material possibilities (access to time, transport, childcare facilities etc.) which are unevenly distributed across the population. Market theorists tend overall to assume either that the disposition towards choice is generalized across the population or that differences are insignificant. Within the culture of choice British politicians have tended to blame the family – poor choosers are taken to be bad parents. As Edwards and Whitty (1990) suggest, the ideology of the market is built upon a model of 'ideal parenting' and treats the 'ideal' parent as the average parent. Again this is not a neutral effect; rather it is a particular value position and a particular vision of parenting which is constructed to serve the ideology of the market and the culture of choice. Even if we leave aside the values of choice it is also the case that market advocates fail to take up the implications of important variations in access to choice and the impact of the costs of choice, and different capacities to participate in or benefit from the culture of choice – that is, to 'decipher and manipulate complex structures' (Bourdieu and Passeron 1990: 73). The education market presupposes 'possession of the cultural code required for decoding the objects displayed' (pp. 51–2). The market in education is a new cultural, arbitrary and relational concept between the education system and social classes – a new mode of articulation (Connell *et al.* 1982).

The ideology of the market actually works as a mechanism of class reproduction in several interrelated ways. First, it assumes that the skills and predisposition to choice, and cultural capital which may be invested in choice, are generalized. 'Within the marketplace all are free and equal, differentiated only by their capacity to calculate their self-interest' (Ranson 1990: 15). Second, it legitimates differences in these by labelling non-choosers and poor choosers as 'bad parents'. Now neither policy nor procedures are to blame, the chooser is at fault, the biases in the system are obscured, 'because in matters of culture absolute dispossession excludes awareness of being dispossessed' (Bourdieu and Passeron 1990: 210). By 'imposing misrecognition of the dominant arbitrary' (p. x), the market produces exclusion and disqualification through a language of empowerment. Third, the education market doubly disadvantages the 'poor chooser' (and the minority chooser) by linking the distribution of resources to the distribution of choices. A system of exclusion and differentiation is created which reasserts and ramifies the relative advantages of the middle and upper classes within state education.

The role of cultural capital in relation to choice is both general and specific. It is general in the sense that certain types and amounts of cultural, social and economic capital are required in order to be an active and strategic chooser: for example, knowledge of local schools, access to and the ability to read and decipher significant information, the ability to engage with and decipher the 'promotional' activities of schools (like open evenings, brochures and videos), the ability to maximize choice by 'working the system' (making multiple applications, applying for scholarships etc.) and the ability to engage in activities involving positive presentation of self (e.g. when meeting key gatekeepers). It is specific in the sense that the making of 'successful' choices, getting your first choice, can depend upon direct engagement, advocacy and pursuit of your choice. There are *key points of articulation* in the choice process, when certain kinds of cultural and social capital are crucial: for example, in the case of oversubscribed schools, the capacity to make direct approaches to the school or to follow through the legalistic process of 'appeal' (mounting an effective case).[2] Whitty *et al.* (1989) demonstrate the same mix of class advantage and class opportunism in take-up of the assisted places scheme. And analysis of families participating in the Milwaukee Parental Choice Program (Witte 1993) indicates many similarities to those in the APS study. And similar factors may be at work in the obtaining of places at CTCs; Dale (1989a: 14) argues that for successful applicants, 'a CTC place for their child is a reward for parental commitment to family, self-improvement, initiative and deservingness'.

An inability or unwillingness to participate in these aspects of 'choosing' or an ignorance of them among certain class groups is a form of what Bourdieu and Passeron call 'self exclusion' – based in part perhaps upon a belief that the system does not work for them. And there is a further dimension to self-exclusion and to the discriminatory effects of the culture of choice. The system of choice presupposes a set of values which gives primacy to comparison, mobility and long-term planning; it ignores those cultures which give primacy to the values of community and locality. The social and geographical horizons of stable communities may be limited and the proximity and history of the local school may be valued in their own right (see Bowe and Ball with Gold 1992; Ball *et al.* forthcoming; Gewirtz *et al.* 1994a).

As the diversity of schools becomes more complex and as systems of application and admission become more devolved, then the difficulties involved in coping with the system, the possibilities of 'working the system' and the possibilities of abuse all increase. All of this is very evident in Moore and Davenport's (1990) analysis of the development of nascent systems of diversification and choice in New York, Chicago, Boston and Philadelphia. They conclude that: 'Although theorists about public school choice envision choice systems in which students with diverse characteristics have equal access to schools of choice, this ideal was very seldom in evidence in these four cities' (p. 192; see also HMI 1990b). And significantly, in the light of the argument being developed here, they point out that:

> Students ended up in the various types of high schools and programs indicated earlier as the result of a complex admission process that included the following (sometimes overlapping) steps: (1) recruitment and information-gathering, (2) application, (3) screening, (4) selection of students offered places, and (5) final student acceptance. Investigating each step in this process highlights the many points at which formal requirements, informal requirements, staff discretion, and parent and student initiative affected the final result, typically to the detriment of equitable admissions ... An interview study conducted in New York ... confirmed an observation we heard consistently: most students and parents did not understand the high school admissions process ... Those families who took the time and had the connections to master its intricacies were at a major advantage ... Study consultants characterized the admissions process as one in which the successful parent often had to serve as 'advocate and negotiator'.
> (Moore and Davenport 1990: 194, 197)

The USA and the UK

I want to return to the issue of the ideological geography of the education market. It is important here to register some of the current differences which exist between US systems and the UK system.

First, the US systems are stronger on diversification but weaker on choice than the UK system. But certainly where choice exists in the USA middle-class parents make the most of it (Halsey *et al.* (1980: 217) suggest that this was a recurrent feature of educational reform). As regards diversity, the absence of a rigidly imposed curriculum, as in post-1988 Chicago for instance, coupled with parent empowerment and school-based management, does allow for curriculum variation between schools and local decision making in curriculum issues.

Second, the UK is weak on parent empowerment and local control. The governor system in the UK has a superficial resemblance to US systems (local schools councils in Chicago) but is modelled on a business rather than populist/participatory paradigm of control. The UK governors are stronger on financial control but weaker on educational control than their US counterparts and are more limited to issues of delivery and performance monitoring than to innovation and local matching to student needs. As indicated, the Conservative government in the UK is highly suspicious of local democracy and favours a consumer–school relationship. Concomitantly, the UK system of LMS is finance-led; that is, headteachers and senior managers in the schools become primarily budget/market/income-oriented (see Chapters 4 and 5).

Third, the UK system of market schooling has no commitment to social goals of equality or justice embedded within it: the Conservative government is firmly set against such notions. Most US metropolitan systems do have significant commitments to these issues, e.g. desegregation and low-income/special need funding (as in Chicago). Indeed, the direction of change in the reform processes is exactly the opposite in this respect when comparing the UK and the US systems. In the UK the funding system, based heavily on school enrolment numbers, is squeezing out special need funding and has the effect of redirecting funding away from existing special needs facilities and services. In contrast, in Chicago the post-1988 restructuring has had as one of its aims the redirection of State Chapter 1 funds to low-income students. 'Beginning in the school year 1989–90 and phased over four years, 100% of the State Chapter 1 funds will follow the students who generate them' (Chicago School Reform Act). This is being achieved (Hess 1992). In relation to UK funding, Lee (1991: 24–5) records:

Under LMS, schools may attempt to limit the intake of pupils who are potentially 'expensive' unless they are specifically and adequately funded by the LEA . . . However, even if the formula provides generously for special needs this does not guarantee that children's particular needs will be met because those funds cannot be earmarked by the LEA for specific purposes.

In other words, special needs funds are both being reduced and being disconnected from those who have such needs. The actual allocations of funds specifically related to special needs are limited by government and vary enormously between LEAs.

Conclusions

Why has the market alternative attracted so much political support from both left and right? There is a basic conundrum facing sociologists of education in the analysis of policies of choice which Orfield (1990: 123) points up: 'Why are some policies seen as successes without evidence and others dismissed as failures even when there was some evidence of their success?' How then should we understand the market sociologically?

In the debate about parental choice issues related to defining the social purposes of public schooling become obscured, to say the least. The market solution, that choice will satisfy both individual families and the nation, seems little more than an act of faith. Much greater attention needs to be paid to the relationships between individual wants and national interests, as well as to those between efficiency and equity and generally those between the economic and social purposes of education. Boyd (1982: 122) noted some time ago that 'Solutions are elusive precisely because the public desires that the public schools be simultaneously efficient, equitable and responsive to consumers.' The market does not change that policy conundrum and there is a degree of logical perversity in arguments which suggest that national economic needs and requirements will be served better by a system of individual choice and deregulation than by state planning; unless we accept that these needs and requirements are met 'automatically' as side-effects of the 'state of families'. However, the National Curriculum lobbies in the USA and UK would indicate that there is a lack of political confidence in the side-effects thesis. Underlying all of this is the assumption that individual (and national) 'needs' and individual 'wants' are the same thing. But there is no clear argument in market theory to support this fusion. As we have seen, in the UK this problem is, in a sense, solved by the government taking on the role of articulating parental wants in its requirements for market information from schools (the Parents' Charter and the 1993 Education Act). I have already noted the mismatch between the government's conception of these wants and those expressed by parents in research studies.[3]

If there is so little evidence to support the claims made for the market by its advocates, and if there is enough counter-evidence to be at least decently sceptical, why does it continue to attract support from policy makers? Clune (1990: 395) argues that

> choice might serve as a powerful means of political legitimation, shifting responsibility for results from the system to its clients (e.g. students and parents), satisfying one of education's most demanding and powerful political clients, American business, and cloaking the system in the powerful American Ideology of consumer sovereignty and entrepreneurial competition.

In fact the unchecked movement between the arguments about needs and wants provides for two different modes of legitimation via the market mode: greater liberty and the raising of national standards. Furthermore, as Weiss (1993) and Clune (1990) argue, the replacing of state planning by market forces, as the organizing principle for the education system, provides a neat and powerful solution to the existing crisis of legitimation in education.

I believe these to be important reasons but want to add to them the argument that choice and the market provide a way for the middle classes to reassert their reproduction advantages in education, which had been threatened by the increasing social democratic de-differentiation of schools, the cultural reform of the curriculum (the elimination of this cultural arbitrary) and the diversion of resources to those with greatest learning needs and difficulties. Choice and the market reassert those privileges, which confer on the privileged 'the supreme privilege of not seeing themselves as privileged' (Bourdieu and Passeron 1990: 210).

Furthermore, interwoven and ramified by the class differentials of the market there is a fractioning along ethnic, religious and gender lines. The data from Moore and Davenport clearly show the exclusionary effects of systems of selection and choice in terms of racial segregation and discrimination. Thus, the market provides a mechanism for the reinvention and legitimation of hierarchy and differentiation via the ideology of diversity, competition and choice.

Moore and Davenport (1990: 221) conclude that 'Public school choice is a reform strategy whose advocates have thus far failed to prove that it can bring about the widespread school improvement that is essential in the nation's big cities. School choice has proven risks and unproven benefits form students at risk, and has typically represented a new and more subtle form of discriminatory sorting.' The effects of this are addressed by Whitty (1991), who argues that, in the UK, 'current reforms would seem to relate to a version of post-modernity that emphasises "distinction" and "hierarchy" within a fragmented social order, rather than one that positively celebrates "difference" and heterogeneity' (p. 20); and that 'This will have particular consequences for the predominantly working class and black populations who inhabit the inner cities. While they never gained an equitable share of educational resources under social democratic policies, the abandonment of planning in favour of the market seems unlikely to provide a solution' (pp. 19–20). David (1992) arrives at the same conclusion in a careful review of policy and research literature, and Carlen *et al.* (1992) paint a bleak picture of increasing class-related inequality in education in a study of schooling and social welfare in the UK midlands. In effect, we have to understand the market as a system of exclusion.

I am not suggesting that all the issues I have raised here are totally ignored by market theorists or PCTs (especially not the latter) but I do suggest that in making either/or arguments about public monopolies versus markets the over-generalized deficiencies of the former and the idealized strengths of the latter are systematically highlighted. Writing in 1982, Boyd made the crucial point, and it remains the crucial point:

> it appears, from the broader perspective of political economy, that a reliance entirely upon private schools would be likely to increase social segregation and inequities within our pluralistic society. The challenging task at present is thus the invention of social arrangements that avoid the dangers of both market failure and non-market failure (i.e. the pathologies of public monopolies).
>
> (Boyd 1982: 123)

All this must not lead us to forget the entrenched inequalities that already existed in the education systems of the UK and the USA or to romanticize public monopoly education. 'There is a powerful

resonance in assertions that contrast the benefits of being a consumer in a free market with the dependence and subordination
implied by being a client, patient, tenant or pupil in a professionally
dominated and often patronizing, sexist and racially biased public
service' (Cox 1992: 23–4). Thus, it would be naive and dangerous
to ignore the forms of 'choice', advantage and selection which
operated inside the public monopoly system. 'By concentrating on
the ways in which the operation of the market will be "distorted" by
pre-existing inequalities, we marginalize the extent to which the
pre-existing market has constructed the inequalities' (Power 1992).
We must not, in other words, 'entrap ourselves in the sticky sweet
lies of nostalgia' (Yeatman 1993: 9).

However, the introduction of the market form and its attendant
values and rhetorics into education now legitimates and supports
such bases of inequity, and the struggles within public monopoly
education, however limited they were, to achieve great equity and
social justice are now de-legitimated. Equity is off the agenda, inequality is a cornerstone of the market. The question as to whether
patterns of relative advantage overlay absolute improvement for all
within the education market is difficult to answer clearly. But the
uneven distribution of resources between schools and the 'creative
destruction' of the change processes and disciplines of the market
suggest that some students will be losing out and some will be less
well supported than they would have been previously. Furthermore,
insofar as education operates as a positional good, for example in
relation to labour market entry or access to higher education, and
where increases in the supply of appropriately qualified candidates
results in 'certification inflation', then it is relative advantage that is
important: 'where educational expansion overcrowds superior positions as a whole . . . the effect will be to push competition by hitherto
qualified applicants down the hierarchy of jobs: screening will be
intensified at each level' (Hirsch 1977: 50). Here education becomes

> a defensive necessity to private individuals even if there are no
> net social returns to education . . . Education becomes a good
> investment not because it would raise an individual's income
> above what it would have been if no one had increased there
> education, but because it raises their income above what it will
> be if others acquire an education and they do not.
>
> (Thurow and Douglas 1972: 38)

A free market enables those who seek education as a defensive necessity to use their social, economic and cultural advantages in an unfettered way to sustain and maintain their position.

The available evidence indicates that we are moving towards a socially deformed market, marked by class biases, mediated by the endogenous demands of cultural capital and the exogenous effects of social and economic disadvantage. Saunders (1986: 331) argues that

> The point, then, is that the different modes of consumption offer different capacities for control, but that the ability to take advantage of these reflects other dimensions of power and inequality in our society, of which gender is one. And as Weber was well aware, a change in one dimension of power has no necessary implications as regards a change in any other.

In both the USA and the UK there is evidence of and further potential for social stratification and differentiation in the education systems. Arguably, it is already possible in the UK to point to the redistribution of resources towards the more able students. There certainly is evidence of the movement of resources *away* from those with learning difficulties (Lee 1991). And explanations of difference in experience of the market may increasingly be aimed at parents and families themselves (a new form of social pathology) rather than the operation of the market itself. All these elements combine to gear public education more directly than previously to the reproduction of social and economic inequalities. The market works as a class strategy by creating a mechanism which can be exploited by the middle classes as a strategy of reproduction in their search for relative advantage, social advancement and mobility.

Notes

1 I am indebted to my colleagues Sharon Gewirtz, Richard Bowe and Alan Cribb, and Barry Troyna, Manfred Weiss and two referees for their contributions to the arguments in this chapter. The chapter also benefited from ongoing discussions with Richard Bowe and Sharon Gewirtz related to two research projects: one funded by the Strategic Research Fund of King's College; the other funded by the Economic and Social Research Council, Grant No. 232858.

2 Adler *et al.* (1989: 144–54) describe in graphic detail the conduct of appeals hearings in Scotland, and the social and linguistic skills demanded

are clear. There are parallels to be drawn with Moore and Davenport's (1990: 197) analysis of 'successful' parents as 'advocate and negotiator'.

3 A different resolution of the national needs conundrum lies in the argument that the insertion of the market into education provides the basis for a new 'correspondence' (Bowles and Gintis 1975) between the school and the sub-structures of the post-Fordist economy (see Ball 1990b: Chapter 5).

8

Competitive schooling: values, ethics and cultural engineering

Introduction

Schools in England and Wales are now set within the whole para-phernalia of a market system, albeit a market which is strongly politically regulated. The universalist, collectivist orientation of comprehensive education is being replaced by a diverse and selective, competitive and atomistic school system. The framework of market discipline is set by parental choice, open enrolment, devolved budgets and per capita funding;[1] but this only bites upon schools in areas where the market is animated by surplus places and geographical propinquity, and thus effective competition for students. This chapter reports on research conducted in one such metropolitan/suburban area extending across two local education authorities.[2]

None of the fifteen secondary schools in this study can afford to ignore the market place. While some are better placed than others, being oversubscribed, there is an awareness that there is a degree of volatility and fashion in parental choice. In interviews conducted with headteachers the need 'not to be complacent' was pointed up by everyone. None the less, the logic of the market suggests that those schools which are oversubscribed or working more or less at full capacity have less reason to change what they are currently doing, or at least to rethink radically their current practice, than those schools currently significantly undersubscribed. They are, in general terms at least, satisfying their consumers. However, the research clearly indicates that it is a mistake to see patterns of choice as being solely an expression of educational preference in any simple sense. There is no *simple* relationship between enrolment and quality, as some advocates of choice would have us believe. What might be called the 'accidents' of the market, as well as the effects of 'market planning', bring extraneous factors into play. Examples of the first are geography and demography – some 'good' schools are difficult to get to or serve declining populations. An example of the second is the opening of a new school adjacent to an old, with the effect of diverting enrolments. Furthermore, it is not clear that schools in the market place are oriented to or responsive to either the needs or the wants of parents in any *simple* sense.

Given the above, the main concerns of this chapter are: (a) to illustrate some aspects of difference in ways that schools participate in the market, and (b) to cast some light upon the responsiveness of schools, and thus the meaning and effects of responsiveness (see conclusion). Woods (1992: 207) defines responsiveness in technicist terms. That is:

- whether schools are making changes as a result of choice and heightened competition and, if so, whether such changes are substantive (to do with policies, practices, curriculum, organisation and the like) rather than concerned only with image and activities aimed at promoting the school.
- whether such changes result in schooling which more closely accords with parental wishes (related to this how school decision makers decide what changes to make and, in particular, how they assess what parents look for in a school or what innovations might attract parents).

But I am most preoccupied here with the value changes and ethical dilemmas provoked by market activity and competition. That is the *moral environment* of the market. Chapter 7 examined the morality *of* the market (in the sense of its outcomes and sociological consequences); this chapter examines the morality *in* the market (in the sense of changes in attitude and behaviour).

The introduction of the market form is typically described and justified by its advocates as the replacement of partisan planning and producer capture by the neutral mechanism of consumer choice. However, this kind of abstract formulation diverts attention away from the ensemble of values and ethics embedded in and required for the 'effective' implementation of the market form. In particular,

I want to argue that the market and neo-liberalism, the political theory upon which it is based, celebrate the ethics of what Nagel (1991) calls the 'personal standpoint' – the personal interests and desires of individuals – and obscure and deprecate the egalitarian concerns of the 'impersonal standpoint'. What Nagel calls 'the duality of standpoints' and sees as the basis for practical ethics and moral stability – that is, the nexus of equality and partiality – is thus collapsed. Markets variously rely upon or encourage social psychologies of hedonism or self-interest. In theory at least, personal motives are given absolute preference over impersonal values. 'Happiness is confused with mere pleasure, and private interest is treated as the principle purpose in life' (Benton 1992: 114). Within the market form both consumers and producers are encouraged, by the rewards and punishments of 'market forces', and legitimated, by the values of the personal standpoint, in their quest for positional advantage over others, what Kenway (1990 p. 155) calls the 'cult of selfishness' (see also Lowery *et al.* 1992, on public and private spheres). The idea of the deliberate and planned pursuit of the 'common good' is rendered meaningless. We can already see these market values, and the 'deformed ethics' to which they give rise, at work in the UK school system (see Ball *et al.* 1993a):

> the advocates of the enterprise culture are seeking, quite deliberately to change the parameters within which arguments about the morality of the market may take place; that they hope to change the moral environment within which market power and market outcomes are judged.
>
> (Marquand 1992: 68–9)

Leadership – hawks, doves and agnostics

In the ensemble of reforms affecting schools as a result of the 1988 Education Reform Act the role and power of the headteacher have been highlighted and enhanced (see Chapter 6). The model for headship implied by the Act is that of chief executive and the mode of engagement with staff and decision making is that of commercial managerialism (see Chapters 4 and 5). Concomitantly, the working conditions, conditions of service and work relationships of classroom teachers were also changed. In effect, management and the market are complimentary and mutually reinforcing aspects of educational reform.

The headteacher therefore plays the key role in setting the agenda for school participation in the market, although the attitudes and values of school governors are also important (see Gewirtz *et al.* 1993). The headteachers in this study take up a variety of value stances towards the education market and these stances have implications for practice. Here, I will refer to three heads: Mrs Carnegie (a hawk), Mr Bracewell (a dove) and Mrs Alison (an agnostic). It is important to underline the heuristic status of these categories. They are fairly rough and ready and the stances of the three headteachers might certainly be characterized as different degrees of unease with the market and market values. Furthermore, the discussion is most definitely focused upon the *morality of actions* rather than the *morality of persons*. I will present, first of all, the 'positions' articulated by these heads and then relate these to some particular policies and events. It must be acknowledged that the development and application of a 'grounded' analysis of ethics and values is not easy; the commentary offered below should be regarded as tentative rather than definitive. Finally, the exclusive focus on headteachers here is not intended to suggest that neither governors nor teachers are involved 'in the market' or confronted by value dilemmas. The focus on heads is an analytical tactic. The descriptions of the schools are deliberately somewhat vague.

Mr Bracewell's and Mrs Carnegie's schools are grant maintained; Mrs Alison's school is LEA funded. Mr Bracewell's school is under-subscribed, the other two are oversubscribed. All three are desig-nated as comprehensive schools. The three schools were chosen to highlight differences in the impact of and response to the disciplines of the market.

The heads

Mrs Carnegie sees it as necessary to come to grips with the inescap-able realities of the market in order to do the best for her school.

> I think one has to be very firm actually, if you want comprehen-sive education to survive here at all you have to be as hawkish as they are. I don't really feel that I'm affecting other schools that I value, like Hutton or Milton or Trumpton, they're three schools that I value, and I think that there's room enough for us all. And we feel that as heads. We meet quite regularly as a

group of heads, the grant maintained heads, and we don't really feel we threaten one another. In fact it's quite a joke, because we say 'Ah! There's a bit of good practice, we'll pinch that from you.' So we know we take from one another, and yet we have to maintain a different ethos, I think. You couldn't be more different than Milton and us [this difference is explored below].

She is uncertain about competition but was clear in interview that in practical terms she has few qualms about pursuing policies which might effect the survival of those schools she does not value (she named two). She also sees the development and maintenance of a distinct identity within the market as a key factor in achieving a competitive edge. But she continues:

Competition I find a bit harder really to come to terms with ... but at the end of the day I think one has to accept it's competitive, but I'm not so happy with that idea. I'd prefer to think from my own point of view about it being conveying a certain model of a school which people can like or choose to take or not to take. And of course that does come down to being in competition ... One of our reactions now is we're having a glossy prospectus next year. We are actually no longer having a home grown prospectus. And I think looking at the marketing of sixth form, which is a new departure in the market, we've got to move in that direction for the sixth form, because there's a lot of competition here, from colleges and neighbourhood institutions. I think we will gradually be spending more money on marketing.[3]

Thus, Mrs Carnegie is not without doubts but sees it as an undeniable necessity that she take competition and the market very seriously. She is looking for new markets in which to participate and is willing to spend money on active 'marketing'. The parallels with business methods and the use of entrepreneurial skills are clear.

Mr Bracewell finds it less easy to accept the need to market his school, but his stand is not unequivocal:

I don't like all this marketing stuff, and I don't think that's what the job is. That's to say, it's not that I'm uncomfortable within it, which I am, it's that I think that it's wrong headed, and that what schools need to be doing isn't, as it were, promoting themselves, but presenting themselves.

Mr Bracewell's distinction between promotion and presentation may be a fine one but it does have implications for how the school conducts itself in the market place. He is much more reluctant than Mrs Carnegie to accept marketing and competition as inevitable. His language and tone are both more careful and more hesitant.

It may be that in presenting the school, what one did was to draw people's attention to the fact that everybody at this school has a degree. I don't know how you do it, you might put some pictures in the prospectus, but I think it's important, because what it means is that you are presenting what you are, rather than trying to be something you're not. And you might call that just semantics. I think that's helpful to people like me and schools like this and also that's, in a way, that's about saying that state schools are good, and this is one of them.

Mr Bracewell was asked how far he would be willing to go in market terms to ensure the survival of his school.

In Robert Bolt's play Thomas More makes a point to Richard Rich about arguing with the devil or something, and he says, well if you break all the rules, and you're arguing with the devil and you suddenly look round behind you and there aren't any [rules]. Well I think the same is true, isn't it. What are you defending, once you renege on the principle? It's a different institution and I don't work in it! I also think, I might be proved wrong, that people sending their children to schools are not as foolish and as easily duped by gloss or by pork pies or whatever.

He seems to be attempting to articulate a language of ethics, of principles, and to relate his practice, albeit again hesitantly, to those principles. And in practical terms the point of difference here seems to be that while Mr Bracewell wants to defend what he sees as the strengths of his school, Mrs Carnegie is embarked on a process of changing aspects of her school in order to ensure its competitiveness. She is proactive in the educational marketplace. Interestingly, as noted already, it is Mrs Carnegie's school that is oversubscribed and Mr Bracewell's that is undersubscribed.

By contrast again, Mrs Alison's position is essentially reactive and pragmatic; she sees the need to respond to her competitors (rather than directly to parents). But there are also similarities here with Mr Bracewell's notion of 'presenting'.

> I think we've got to a stage where marketing, on the one hand,
> it would be very naive not to be aware of it and that you need
> to do X, Y and Z. But, on the other hand, I think that I really
> do feel now, even more than I did before, that you do what's
> right for your school, that you shove things forward, that you
> sell what there is and that's that.

But this stance is clearly related in her own mind to her school being
oversubscribed. She admits that if things were different the luxury of
integrity would be lost. Integrity is conditional.

> If we were in that tight corner, fighting for survival, then I
> think probably you do, rightly or wrongly, put money into glossy
> marketing, which is just more down the end of marketing with
> a capital M rather than a small m. Can you understand the
> shorthand? But we're not in that situation and so we can con-
> tinue keeping our integrity.

This ethical suspicion of 'the market' is echoed by the deputy
head at Mrs Alison's school, who is responsible for liaison with primary
schools.

> Marketing gets mentioned and it always gets mentioned with
> inverted commas round it, you know, we are 'marketing', as it's
> somehow dirty trade to be doing, it's not what we're here for.
> But obviously there's a recognition that if you don't market, if
> you don't sell what's good about your school you're not going
> to actually fill your school.
>
> (Mr Duke)

Mrs Alison also feels that local authority primary transfer policies
have disadvantaged her school and have necessitated greater energy
and expenditure being devoted to marketing than she would really
want: 'and we actually had to put a lot more energy into marketing, which disadvantages kids in your own school, what you might
have wanted to do in your own school.' Clearly, for Mrs Alison the
market won't go away, competition must be taken seriously: 'your
marketing isn't just what's happening in your own school, it's what's
happening in other schools, because if other people are doing things
and you're not then that gives a message about you, that you didn't
create, but it's there.' In particular, Mrs Alison's senior management
team (SMT) is very aware of and quick to react to the activities of its
nearest competitor, Lockmere School.

Well they're the school that is more aggressive than other schools. We feel it quite keenly, because we, because of our position and so on, are in competition perhaps with Lockmere whereas we're not with Fletcher, for example. They are more aggressive, and it is felt that there is more of a 'sell' rather than a reflection of the truth. Now I think that's partly wrong, actually, but that is the perception and they're certainly . . . I will alter some of the things that I say and do when I go out to schools, knowing that Lockmere has spoken to various junior schools that I have. I mean last year at this time, and it happens in the autumn term is when all the aggro comes out really, because that's when people are panicking about not going to have enough kids for the following year, when it's all happening . . . Lockmere had a policy of going into schools and doing a very hard sell. They went into a school that we always tradition-ally went into. And people referred to it as the Lockmere Road Show.

The language is again interesting. Here, 'aggression' and 'panic' are terms which point up the combative and emotive nature of the market place. There seems to be little space here for the niceties of principle and integrity. What is happening is not so much a simple respon-siveness to parents, to consumers, but also part of the dynamic of the market which arises from emulation of and rivalry with competitor institutions. Indeed, Mr Duke, one of Mrs Alison's deputy heads, sees little evidence of the school adapting to parental pressures of concerns.

I can't think of any. I suspect there might be some subtle changes and so on. I suppose actually putting out a weekly newsletter is a change, to make sure that they are better in-formed . . . We've done changes to the school journal's policy, as a result of comments that have come through individual parents and the PTA . . . it tends to be on the social pastoral side, communication side, as opposed to perhaps the academic side.

None the less, professional decision making is now set within a dif-ferent frame of reference.

There's been a change in people, putting forward views: 'I think we want to do it this way, what will parents think about that; can we sell that to parents without . . . ?; what arguments might they bring up against it?'

Parents, or the *abstract* parent (but not the *general* parent), are now the point of reference in the vocabulary of decision making. That is to say, not all parents are seen as 'competent consumers' (or desirable clients).

> I certainly think when choosing a school that they know what they want actually. But the idea of parents being responsible . . . I think the majority of parents, well certainly about 40, 50 per cent in this country are not very responsible. And we have to raise their expectations of education.
>
> (Mrs Carnegie)

Returning to the question of emulation and rivalry, all this has implications for relationships between schools and specifically for the cooperation between schools in areas like curriculum development or shared sixth forms. It is clear that in both LEAs involved here, in one drastically and in one steadily, histories of cooperation are being weakened. The headteacher of one of Mrs Carnegie's most immediate competitors, Northwark Park School, describes the changes thus:

> When I came with the previous head we were both, we were members of SHA [Secondary Headteachers Association] and we would meet with other schools regularly, again all the schools from Northwark would be represented and they would discuss mutual problems and things. These meetings more or less no longer exist, and if they do they're poorly attended, and I don't think there is any rift between heads as such, but there is not the unity that there was. Maybe there's a feeling of mutual suspicion, you know, and everybody's sort of watching each other very carefully, but I don't see any great sense of cooperation.

The point is that in a situation of competition, with enrolments and therefore budgets at stake, the actions of any one institution have implications for all others. While Mrs Alison is suspicious of Lockmere, schools in competition with her school[4] and with Mrs Carnegie's (see note 3) also find some of their actions hostile and dubious.

> I'm not saying it's lost its comprehensive ideals, but Mrs Carnegie, who is the head there, in my view has set herself up

as near as damn it as a traditional girls' grammar school, and taken on all the trappings and trimmings, the strict uniform, that sort of somewhat autocratic set up as far as the staff are concerned, the very much sort of high profile head, very much in control, that whole sort of ethos and they've gone for that and it seems to have gone down a bomb. I mean it's obviously attracted a lot of people. You know, you can imagine trying to put that across here and I think you might run into difficulties. So I mean it's interesting, whether she did that with the co-operation of the staff or whether that was just decided, she just said well I'm boss, I'm going to do this but sometimes that sort of approach does seem to attract people in.

(Deputy head of Northwark Park)

It is always easy to see someone else as the villain – and Mrs Carnegie has her own opinions about her rival schools accepting LEA money for rebuilding work in exchange for a move to 'magnet' status – but the point is that the market is divisive, it encourages hostility and suspicion, and it provides a vocabulary of motives that serve to justify a value system based upon a belief in the worst in other people. In other words, the market destroys or dissolves some social relations and creates others (Sayers 1992). It rewards shrewdness rather than principle and leads to an emphasis on short-term, self-interested decision making. The change in relationships is taking place within as well as between schools.

There's still some working together, and there's not the competition. But you can see from the beginnings of what happened when we had the budget crisis, people saying we've got to do this, this and this to survive. How do we do it? We've got to do those things to survive. And people are saying, 'how does it actually affect the way I've actually got to teach?'

I think that the commitment of teachers to certain issues, say mixed ability or an issue like comprehensiveness, is a commitment which they would say they believe in, but when it comes down to it, if they were convinced of another argument, they'd follow another one, they're swayable, very swayable, I think. Because they think first and foremost, quite rightly, 'I've got a mortgage to pay. I've got to do something about my mortgage, my kids', or whatever else it is.

(Union representative at Mr Bracewell's school)

If we had wanted to go into industry we'd have gone into industry. Because in industry you're expected to do certain things.
In teaching you're not or you weren't when many people en-
tered the profession, therefore they don't feel it's appropriate,
they certainly don't feel its appropriate for a head to tell them
what to wear.

                    (Union representative at Mrs Carnegie's school)

I do not want to convey the impression here that the market behaviour of schools is simply a matter of different value positions that
people take up and that is all that counts. That is clearly not the
case. The disciplines of the market are very real, the pressures on
headteachers to ensure the survival of their school are very real, the
dilemmas they face are very real. But neither do I accept the view
that responsiveness to patterns of choice in the education market is
the working through of an inevitable and neutral mechanism or the
playing out of simple coercive pressures. Values mediate the market
but the market also has effects on values. There is a *values attrition*
at work whereby the boundaries of 'acceptable' behaviour are con-
stantly being shifted back. Schools have choices about how they participate in the market but those choices are severely limited. The
market cannot be easily ignored. This process of attrition, what is
described elsewhere as values drift (Gewirtz *et al.* 1993), is further
obscured by the assertion of *technocratic managerialism* over and against
what might be termed *ethical professionalism.* The values of and in
school leadership are dramatically shifting away from the latter towards
the former and this adds to the marginalization of values-led debate
within education. Within the former, social relationships are reduced
to the 'merely utilitarian'. The emphasis is upon 'technical as opposed
to substantive rationality: which has the "effect of depoliticising issues"'
(Trotman and Robertson 1992: 73; and see Considine 1988). The
emphasis of technical rationality is upon the development of techniques, procedures and organizational practices which are intended
to facilitate speed of decision making, coordination, the setting and
reviewing of objectives, good financial controls and information, cost
improvement, responsiveness and consumer loyalty. The emphasis of
substantive rationality is upon the intrinsic qualities of the 'product-
process', here education, teaching and learning. For example, the
development of collaborative cultures, participative decision making
and educative leadership would be central to the discourse of school
organization.

Presentation, promotion and response

Earlier I quoted Mr Bracewell's distinction between promotion and presentation. In a sense the first is about imagery and the second is about advocacy. The difference is probably most clear-cut in the positions articulated by Mr Bracewell and Mrs Carnegie. In Mr Bracewell's interview the tone, as regards market involvement, was very much defensive, representing what is called elsewhere *reluctant implication* (Gewirtz *et al.* 1993). In Mrs Carnegie's interview the tone was much more assertive, promotional and responsive, representing what might be termed *positional exploitation.* She displays at least some of the characteristics that Ralston (1990) identifies with the 'academic entrepreneur'. Let us offer some examples of the latter.

> Staff here didn't want uniform, and really made very clear their views that they didn't want uniform, but on a survey of parents they did and therefore we went for uniform. So that was certainly responding to the consumer. Another thing is we've done a survey of why parents chose this school and one of the things that comes high is security and discipline, and so therefore, though ourselves actually by about year nine, we would have liked to let them off site, we have decided that we will keep them on the site, and that's a very powerful thing with parents . . .

> We brought pupils in much more to sell, there's no doubt about that. Pupil involvement, we've changed that as well and I think it's been constantly with me, actually, the marketing of the school . . .

> The principal's got a hard job really in establishing – they call it the image of the school – but in another way you could call it marketing. And this is a good thing, and something that will really be influential in bringing the right sort of parents into this school, and stick with it. And we have some very powerful governors and their bottom line was very clearly, the school will continue to be comprehensive. But I think we're thinking of all sorts of ways – how do we enhance the comprehensive image? *The image that anyone could get in and therefore they could do what they like,* basically, when they get here. And we have to fight, I think, against that all the time. (Emphasis added)

> Our image I think is fairly clear. The senior team actually has given a lot of thought to it, and particularly some members

whose interest it is. And I think is a pretty secure image. I mean
we have a statement, like all schools now, 'Today's education
for the women of tomorrow.' And that is something short and
snappy, but it does encapsulate all sorts of things here, like our
equal opportunities policy. We do have a school logo, which is
pupil designed . . .

How do we safeguard comprehensive education? And one of
the things is, we've had this school agreement this year, which
has expectations of the school and the parents, and the pupils,
and I think this is rather interesting. I think what we'll be
looking to a year from now is to say that parents are expected
to sign this agreement *before an offer of a place is made.* (Emphasis
added)

Now there are a number of points of interest and contradiction
here. All of this is set within Mrs Carnegie's commitment to comprehensive education:

I believe that Mrs Carnegie is firmly in favour of comprehensive education, you know, taking everybody. But if it was a different head who didn't have these strong feelings, then that's
where you might get a change.

(Second year teacher)

None the less, there is a tension here between a commitment to
comprehensive education and the idea that her school should not
be seen as a school that 'anyone can get into' or a school that offers
places to students on certain conditions. I would also underline the
development of corporate imagery (logo, motto, distinctive uniform,
school flag). And note the privileging of parental views over and
above those of the school staff (see Chapter 6). There is also a
crucial aspect of the dynamic of the education market in the UK
being highlighted here. If a school wishes to improve its image and
performance in the market place then among the most effective
strategies are (a) to recruit more students who are likely to perform
well academically, and (b) to exclude students who are likely not to
do well academically. Whether this can be seen as related to raising
standards is problematic. In effect, students are both consumers *and*
commodities in the education market and they carry value based not
simply upon the income they generate but also upon their ability/
potential as test and examination fodder. Again, these are important

issues of values. Here it is possible to identify transgression of what Plant (1992) sees as one of the basic general principles which might be articulated to impose boundary limits on extension of the market; that is, 'the idea of respect for persons: that people themselves should not be treated as commodities, or as means to the ends of others' (p. 92). The logic (and effect) of this kind of market-related selection is that undersubscribed schools will recruit (in part by default) more students designated as 'less able' and have a smaller budget to use in their education. The national rise in the number of exclusions from school and the dismantling of SEN (special educational needs) support (see Gewirtz *et al.* 1993) can be subject to a similar kind of analysis. The actions taken by schools in the market place to ensure survival raise important questions about the respect for persons which the values of the market displace and obscure. What is right in the market is whatever seems necessary to ensure survival.

The deputy head of Northwark Park School, an undersubscribed competitor of Mrs Carnegie's school, is very much aware of the effects of the market on both recruitment/exclusion and resource allocation. Again it is important to note the way in which the logic of the market displaces *values talk*. The discourse of competition excludes the lexicon of values. In particular, key values associated with (if not always enacted within) *comprehensive education* are displaced (Daunt 1975). Within the moral tradition of comprehensive education values are explicit and education-based, whereas within the market they are heavily implicit and derivative.

> My own view is that in a sense the pressure on schools to produce the goods in terms of academic success has made them less willing to spend their resources and their time and their energy on students who . . . almost dissipate their energies on students who are just trying to mess the system up and I think this will be one of the more noticeable effects of LMS generally, as schools will become less tolerant of those students who do not fit very easily into the pattern of things, whether it's because of their behaviour, may even be whether it's because of their abilities.
>
> (Deputy head)

Clearly, Mrs Carnegie's management team take the market very seriously indeed. What distinguishes Mr Bracewell's school from hers in these respects is the relative absence of changes in policy or practice

that seem to be market related. Mr Bracewell's school has also opted
for grant-maintained status. This is presented as a tactical move to
escape from the anti-comprehensive policies of the LEA. What distinguishes Mr Bracewell's school from Mrs Carnegie's, and most other
grant-maintained schools, is its new school title. It styles itself as *a grant
maintained comprehensive school.* Whatever market advantage that could
accrue from being grant-maintained might well be cancelled out by
the highlighting of comprehensive. And the school appears to take
a much lower profile position in marketing itself. Thus, it is now the
only secondary school in Northwark not to require a uniform from
its students. Mr Bracewell explains:

> We have the notion in school, I hope it's in the school, it's
> certainly in the senior team, in planning and so on, which we
> call issues of principle and value. It's partly ironic, but even
> though you can be ironic about it what it means is that you
> don't rush in to do ten ton of glossy, you do a good . . . you do
> the best possible open evening that you can do, I take a lot of
> care about it. But that's one of our issues of principle and
> value, I don't want to run into glossy stuff. I say to the parents,
> the prospectus is not posh, there's nothing wrong with a glossy
> thing . . . I think what the school is saying to itself is: how do we
> do it within the principles and values of the school? Also in
> terms of pragmatism, you don't want any kind of balloon busi-
> ness, you don't want to suddenly go up market, and bombard
> people with mailshots and who knows what else. I mean we do
> a reasonable prospectus, we do what I take to be quite a nice
> little simple foldover thing – what we stand for. We advertise in
> the local press, we advertise our sixth form in the local press,
> a discreet advert, yes we do that. It's a bit rudimentary, I sup-
> pose, but yes, of course we do, of course we do . . .
>
> So now we have an act of worship every day and we have
> many more whole school assemblies and all of that but that's
> not about getting kids, that's about corporate values.
>
> *SJB*: Mmm . . . I mean that's about looking at yourselves, have
>   you moved to actually looking at your competitors and
>   thinking about them in relation to you, like the CTC and
>   Fletcher?
>
> No, we haven't done that, perhaps we should, we haven't . . . no,
> we haven't done that. We're not a very entrepreneurial school.

Given Mr Bracewell's school's difficult market position, the emphasis on principles rather than shrewdness could be seen as naive. It certainly highlights the pressures that are brought to bear on practice and principle when recruitment is directly related to income. The jobs of those who work in the school are at stake in all this. Within the school the union representative is aware that things are beginning to change.

> [The new floor mats are] by the door as you come in, big blue ones with a red giraffe on it. It's sort of like the corporate image bit. People think it stinks, it's marketing, it's distasteful, and it's something that we never used to go in for. We've always said, you take us as we are, and now it's going for the marketing bit. All the glossy stuff that's pushed out. People think that the media resources officer has got better things to do . . . People feel that marketing is a necessary evil, but they see the best way to do it is low key way to do it.

Arguably virtually all schools are being inducted into what Plant (1992: 87) calls a 'culture of self-interest' and Mr Bracewell's school is not exempt from this. None the less, at face value, the responses of the two schools do appear to be distinct. Mr Bracewell's, perhaps, represents an example of what McLaughlin (1991: 38) calls 'reorientation change', 'which would involve absorption of the language of the market but in such a way that it would make little or no impact on the dominant culture and core working arrangements of the organisation.' And Mrs Carnegie's represents what he calls 'colonization change', which 'involves major shifts in the cultural core of the organization and all its existing forms of actions and activities.' This kind of change is associated with and facilitated by the development of a managerialist style of organizational control and relationships (see Chapters 4 and 5).

The use of the terms 'principle and value' here, and 'integrity' by Mrs Alison earlier, are at least interesting – in that they show an awareness of (the need for/existence of) a moral underpinning to participation in the market. While, on the one hand, the integrity of teachers probably maintains a set of self-governed limits to market behaviour, on the other, market disciplines and incentives erode the limits of integrity. Integrity within teaching is very much a product of normative/collective professionalism and yet both market theory and current government policy in the UK are hostile to collective

professionalism. Thus, in terms, again, of values and ethics the responses of all three heads might be characterized as increasingly
more instrumental and less principled, where 'principled attitudes
involve strong attachment to behavioural norms and instrumental
attitudes involve relative detachment, in which behaviour is regarded
as a neutral means to an end' (Podgorecki 1974). In a different
vocabulary we might see Mr Bracewell as engaged in 'strategic compromise'; 'involving a mixture of internalised adjustment and strategic redefinition' (Sikes *et al.* 1985: 236).

Conclusion

What is being lost, I suggest, from and *in* UK education is any kind
of discourse of civic virtue or social ethics. The majesty of the market
is so stridently trumpeted by its advocates that all else is in danger
of being drowned out. Plant (1992) sees enormous dangers, in general terms, in the 'culture of self-interest' coming to predominate
over and erode the moral underpinnings necessary to the efficiency
and effectiveness of the market itself.

> Without some sense of civic virtue, or orientation to values
> which are not of a self-regarding kind, market behaviour will
> require growing regulation in the interests of the market itself.
> Such regulation, in turn, may become increasingly problematic
> if there is not some more general concern to cultivate a sense
> of social and civic responsibility, which, as I have suggested,
> may become more and more difficult with the erosion of social
> values in favour of private and self-interested ones.
>
> (Plant 1992: 89)

And it is not good enough here simply to point to the practices and
positions taken up by schools or individuals within the education
market place. It is necessary to look to the organization of the market system within which schools are required to operate and the sorts
of rewards and punishments used by government to pursue their
policy preferences (e.g. the use of financial incentives (bribes) to
encourage more schools to opt for grant-maintained status). Within
the existing system of market relations in the UK, self-interest and
individual morality are placed in acute conflict, and self-interest is
privileged in the values of the market. It is the policies that underpin 'ordered competition' that need to be carefully questioned. As
Nagel (1991: 5) argues, 'Even if a market is needed for the efficient

interaction of supply and demand, it is not beyond imagination that some incentive other than personal gain might drive the minimization of costs and the maximization of profits.'

There is a further level of complication in all this which relates back to the pro-market arguments of the New Right and public choice theorists. If, as they argue, the public professions (doctors, teachers, social workers) are motivated by utility maximization rather than any kind of service ethic, then there is no obvious basis for an indigenous system of civic virtue to mitigate the worst excesses of self-interest. If, on the other hand, the service ethic *is* a significant motivation for public professionals, then the reforms like those of interest here may be well on the way to destroying it and replacing it with a culture of self-interest. Thus, Plant (1992: 94) argues that

> in the state sector the introduction of markets, quasi-markets and the dominance of contract might well deprive us of ethic principles such as service and vocation, which are essential to the efficient delivery of services. We have to be very careful about the market again crossing an important moral barrier and replacing one ethic with another.

In substantive terms, within the UK education system there is now a struggle under way over values. I suggest that, at least in recent years, the values of comprehensivism have constituted and provided a language and ethic of civic virtue in education. These are now being destroyed by and replaced by market values. Comprehensive values (Daunt 1975) are essentially an articulation of Nagel's (1991) 'impersonal standpoint' and can be contrasted along several dimensions with the 'culture of self-interest' or 'personal standpoint' represented in market values. As a 'moral tradition' comprehensivism provides a framework for ethical concerns, it articulates a way of life based upon commutarian principles. It provides for a 'thick' morality – shared values and common sentiments. This falls within what Lowery *et al.* (1992) call the 'public sphere', a space in our social world in which issues are open to debate, reflection and moral argument. The market, by contrast, rests on aggregative principles, the sum of individual goods and choices, 'founded on individual and property rights that enable citizens to address problems of interdependence via exchange' (Lowery *et al.* 1992). It provides for a 'thin' morality and generates hierarchy and division based upon competitive individualism (see Figure 8.1).

Figure 8.1

Comprehensive values	*Market values*
individual need (schools and students)	individual performance (schools and students)
commonality (mixed-ability classes/open access)	differentiation/hierarchy (setting/streaming/selection/exclusion)
emphasis on resource allocation to less able	emphasis on resource allocation to more able
collectivism (cooperation between schools and students)	competition (between schools and students)
broad assessments of worth based upon varieties of qualities	narrow assessments of worth based on contributions to performativity
the education of all children is held to be intrinsically of equal worth	the education of children is valued in relation to costs and outcomes

Furthermore, insofar as students are influenced and affected by the hidden curriculum of their institutional environment then the system of morality 'taught' by schools is increasingly well accommodated to the values complex of the enterprise culture. All of this is particularly ironic (or maybe not) given the espoused commitment of the UK government to the development of 'a moral dimension' in schools (DfE 1992: para. 1.29, p. 7). Caught between the state and the market, the school may be on the way to becoming a reflection of and playing its part in reproducing what Kingdom (1992: 1) calls the 'masturbatory society': 'offering a solitary view of fulfilment, free of the complications arising from tiresome moral demands by others.'

In relation to the arguments laid out above, *responsiveness* is a side issue, a matter of empty rhetoric and of ideology. It is an ideological concept. To characterize (and to research) the education market in terms of school responsiveness involves misrecognition of how the market works and ignores and depoliticizes the political project it represents and the moral, value and ethical shifts it contributes to (the abstractions of educational administration and organizational theory so often work their ideological effects in this way). The rhetoric and disciplines of responsiveness are part of a process of 'cultural engineering', of social and political change; part of the assertion of the individualist credo; part of the destruction of the communal ethic. Responsiveness is a smokescreen for self-gratification, for distrust, for competitive individualism, for the ethic of consumption, for social distancing, closure and class advantage. It is the acceptable face of the 'culture of self-interest'. And by focusing attention upon the reactivity of the school in general terms, the idea of responsiveness obscures social patterns of response in relation to race, class and gender differences. Analytically it is important to move beyond the superficialities of the political rhetorics of parental choice and school competition (articulated through concepts like responsiveness) and to begin to explore the social costs incurred and moral depredations wrought in the education market place.

> The highest and most worthy exertions of humanity can flourish only where the intensity of social bonds and civic virtue also flourish. The contrary tendency towards self-interested individual competition can lead only to a debasement of the aims and contents of individual action, and prepare the way for tyranny and despotism.
>
> (Benton 1992: 119)

Notes

1 Parents in England and Wales now have (in theory) complete freedom to choose any state school for their child (in practice this freedom is limited by physical access, selection and oversubscription); 85 per cent of LEA general schools budgets must now be allocated on a strict per capita basis. Thus, actual school budgets are determined primarily by numbers on roll. Schools in many areas therefore compete for choices. Most schools now control and administer their own budget and have considerable autonomy in their expenditure decision making.
2 This is a three-year study of market forces in education funded by the Economic and Social Research Council, grant No. 232858. This chapter is one of several project papers; see also Ball *et al.* (forthcoming), Bowe *et al.* (1993) and Gewirtz *et al.* (1993a, b).
3 Mrs Carnegie is considering expanding the sixth form intake by admitting boys at this level. In terms of competition with neighbouring schools this would be an entirely new departure and might be seen as an example of

what Williamson (1975) calls 'opportunism'; that is the manipulation of the 'rules of the game' to advantage.

4 In preparation for the 1992 student intake the senior management at Mrs Alison's school had, as in previous years, offered places over and above target numbers to take account of non-take-up of places offered (which had been running at about 10 per cent of offers); Mr Duke (deputy head) explained the consequences and the dilemma faced by himself and colleagues: 'This year the drop out initially was not so large . . . And then we had 30 appeals of which 11 were granted. Now those 11 were then added to our numbers and we had 205 coming, when we were actually aiming for 180 . . . there was no way we could have six classes. So we had to go to seven. Now that caused some concern . . . In order to have a seventh class in year seven we needed an extra teacher, in order to have an extra teacher we had to recruit more students . . . We therefore went back to the authority and said, look you've got the list, people on the waiting list, do they still want a place. Because of these set of circumstances we now have some additional places, and some of those people said yes please, and took up the places. Of course, I don't know what effect that had on other schools, I haven't heard. But clearly they were withdrawing from other schools.'

References

Adler, M., Petch, A. and Tweedie, J. (1989). *Parental Choice and Educational Policy*, Edinburgh, Edinburgh University Press.

Alexander, R., Rose, J. and Woodhead, C. (1992). *Curriculum Organisation and Classroom Practice in Primary Schools: a Discussion Paper*, London, Department of Education and Science.

Allan, J. (1990). 'Does feminism need a theory of "the state"?', in Watson, S. (ed.) *Playing the State: Australian Feminist Interventions*, Sydney, Allen and Unwin.

Angus, L. (1994). 'Sociological analysis and educational management: the social context of the self-managing school, *British Journal of Sociology of Education*, 15 (1), 79–92.

Arnott, M., Bullock, A. and Thomas, H. (1992). 'Consequences of local management: an assessment by headteachers. Paper presented to the 8th ERA Research Network Seminar, 12 February.

Aronowitz, S. and Giroux, H. (1991). *Postmodern Education: Politics, Culture and Social Criticism*, Minneapolis, University of Minnesota Press.

Audit Commission (1991). *The Management of Primary Schools*, London, Audit Commission.

Ball, S. J. (1987). *The Micropolitics of the School*, London, Routledge.

Ball, S. J. (1990a). 'Management as a moral technology', in Ball, S. J. (ed.) *Foucault and Education*, London, Routledge.

Ball, S. J. (1990b). *Politics and Policy Making in Education*, London, Routledge.

Ball, S. J. (1990c). 'Markets, inequality and urban schooling', *Urban Review*, 22 (2), 85–100.

Ball, S. J. (1990d). 'Education, inequality and school reform: values in crisis!', Inaugural lecture, King's College, University of London.

Ball, S. J. (1993a). 'Education markets, choice and social class: the market as a class strategy in the UK and US', *British Journal of Sociology of Education*, 14 (1), 3–19.

Ball, S. J. (1993b). 'Education policy, power relations and teachers' work', *British Journal of Educational Studies*, 41 (2), 106–21.

Ball, S. J. (1993c). 'Culture, cost and control: self management and entre-preneurial schooling in England and Wales', in Smyth, J. (ed.) *A Socially Critical View of the Self-managing School*, London, Falmer.

Ball, S. J. (1994). 'Culture, crisis and morality: the struggle over the National Curriculum', in Atkinson, P., Davies, B. and Delamont, S. (eds) *Discourse and Reproduction: Essays for Basil Bernstein*, New York, Hampton Press.

Ball, S. J. and Bowe, R. (1991). 'Micropolitics of radical change: budgets, management and British schools', in Blase, J. (ed.) *The Politics of Life in Schools*, Newbury Park, CA, Sage.

Ball, S. J., Bowe, R. and Gewirtz, S. (1993). 'Schools in the market place: an analysis of local market relations', Paper for the conference on Quasi Markets in Public Sector Service Delivery: the Emerging Findings', Univer-sity of Bristol, School for Advanced Urban Studies.

Ball, S. J., Bowe, R. and Gewirtz, S. (forthcoming). 'Circuits of schooling: a sociological exploration of parental choice in social class contexts', *Socio-logical Review*.

Ball, S. J., Kenny, A. and Gardiner, D. (1990). 'Literacy, politics and the teaching of English', in Goodson, I. and Medway, P. (eds) *Bringing English to Order*, London, Falmer.

Barber, B. (1984). *Strong Democracy*, Berkeley, CA, University of California Press.

Beattie, A. (1987). *History in Peril: May Parents Preserve It*, London, Centre for Policy Studies.

Beilharz, P. (1987). 'Reading politics: social theory and social policy', *Aus-tralia and New Zealand Journal of Sociology*, 23 (3), 388–406.

Benton, T. (1992). 'Adam Fergusons's critique of the "enterprise" culture', in Heelas, P. and Morris, P. (eds) *The Values of the Enterprise Culture: the Moral Debate*, London, Routledge.

Bernstein, B. (1971). 'On the classification and framing of educational knowledge', in Young, M. F. D. (ed.) *Knowledge and Control*, London, Collier-Macmillan.

Bernstein, B. (1990). *The Structuring of Pedagogic Discourse*, London, Routledge.

Blackmore, J. (1990). 'School-based decision-making and teacher unions: the appropriation of a discourse', in Chapman, J. (ed.) *School-based Decision-making and Management*, London, Falmer Press.

Bloom, A. (1987). *The Closing of the American Mind*, New York, Simon and Schuster.

Bourdieu, P. (1986). *Distinction: a Social Critique of the Judgement of Taste*, London, Routledge.

Bourdieu, P. and Passeron, J.-C. (1990). *Reproduction*, London, Sage.

Bowe, R., Ball, S. J. and Gewirtz, S. (1994a). 'Captured by the discourse:

issues and concerns in researching parental choice', *British Journal of Sociology of Education*, 15 (1).

Bowe, R., Ball, S. J. and Gewirtz, S. (1994b). 'Education, consumption and "parental choice"', *British Journal of Educational Studies*, 42 (2).

Bowe, R. and Ball, S. J. with Gold, A. (1992). *Reforming Education and Changing Schools*, London, Routledge.

Bowles, S. and Gintis, H. (1975). *Schooling in Capitalist America*, London, Routledge and Kegan Paul.

Boyd, W. (1982). 'The political economy of future schools', *Educational Administration Quarterly*, 18 (3), 111–30.

Brown, M. (1992). National Curriculum Mathematics – National Evaluation, personal communication.

Brown, P. (1990). 'The "third wave": education and the ideology of parentocracy', *British Journal of Sociology of Education*, 11 (1), 65–86.

Bryant, V. (1991). The exclusion of black schools from London schools, MA in Urban Education dissertation, King's College London, Centre for Educational Studies.

Caldwell, B. and Spinks, J. (1988). *The Self-managing School*, London, Falmer Press.

Carlen, P., Gleeson, D. and Wardhaugh, J. (1992). *Truancy: the Politics of Compulsory Schooling*, Buckingham, Open University Press.

Chubb, J. and Moe, T. (1990). *Politics, Markets and America's Schools*, Washington, DC, The Brookings Institution.

Clarke, K. (1991a). Primary Education: a statement by the Secretary of State for Education and Science, 3 December, London, Department of Education and Science.

Clarke, K. (1991b). Education in a Classless Society. Westminster, Lecture to the Tory Reform Group, 12 June.

Clegg, S. (1989). *Frameworks of Power*, London, Sage.

Clune, W. J. (1990). 'Educational governance and student achievement', in Clune, W. and Witte, J. (eds) *Choice and Control in American Education, Vol. 2*, London, Falmer.

Codd, J. (1988). 'The construction and deconstruction of educational policy documents', *Journal of Education Policy*, 3 (5), 235–48.

Connell, R. W. *et al.* (1982). *Making the Difference*, Sydney, Allen and Unwin.

Considine, M. (1988). 'The corporate management framework as administrative science; a critique', *Australian Journal of Public Administration*, 37 (1), 4–18.

Cookson, Jr, P. W. (1992). 'The ideology of consumerism and the coming deregulation of the public school system', *Journal of Education Policy*, 7 (3), 301–11.

Coopers and Lybrand Deloitte (1992). *The National Union of Teachers: Costs of the National Curriculum in Primary Schools*, London, Coopers and Lybrand Deloitte.

Corwin, R. (1983). *The Entrepreneurial Bureaucracy.* Greenwich, CT, JAI Press.

Cousins, C. (1987). *Controlling Social Welfare.* Brighton, Wheatsheaf.

Cox, D. (1992). 'Crisis and opportunity in health service management', in Loveridge, R. and Starkey, K. (eds) *Continuity and Crisis in the NHS.* Buckingham, Open University Press.

Cuban, L. (1990). 'The fundamental puzzle of school reform', in Lieberman, A. (ed.) *Schools as Collaborative Cultures,* London, Falmer.

Dale, R. (1979). 'The politicisation of school deviance: reactions to William Tyndale', in Barton, L. and Mieghan, R. (eds) *Schools, Pupils and Deviance,* Driffield, Nafferton.

Dale, R. (1989a). 'The Thatcherite project in education: the case of the city technology colleges', *Critical Social Policy,* 9 (3), 4–19.

Dale, R. (1989b). *The State and Education Policy,* Buckingham, Open University Press.

Daunt, P. (1975). *Comprehensive Values,* London, Heinemann.

David, M. (1992). 'Parents and the state: how has social research informed educational reforms', in Arnot, M. and Barton, L. (eds) *Voicing Concerns: Sociological Perspectives on Contemporary Education Reforms,* Wallingford, Triangle.

Davies, M. (1992). 'The little boy said . . . "The Emperor, still isn't wearing any clothes" ', *The Curriculum Journal,* 3 (1), 1–7.

Deal, T. E. (1990). 'Healing our schools: restoring the heart', in Lieberman, A. (ed.) *Schools as Collaborative Cultures,* London, Falmer.

Deem, R. (1990). 'The reform of school governing-bodies: the power of the consumer over the producer?', in Flude, M. and Hammer, M. (eds) *The Education Reform Act 1988,* London, Falmer.

Deem, R. (1992). 'School governing bodies – public concerns and private interests', Paper presented to the International Conference on Accountability and Control in Educational Settings, CEDAR, University of Warwick.

Department for Education (1992). *Choice and Diversity,* London, HMSO.

Department of Education and Science (1988a). *National Curriculum. The Task Group on Assessment and Testing: a Report,* London, HMSO.

DES (1988b). *The Local Management of Schools: Circular 7/88,* London, DES.

DES (1989). *Planning for School Improvement: Advice to Governors, Headteachers and Teachers,* London, DES.

DES (1991a). *Development Planning: a Practical Guide: 2,* London, DES.

DES (1991b). *The Parents' Charter,* London, DES.

Deucher, D. (1989). *The New History. A Critique,* York, The Campaign for Real Education.

Eagleton, T. (1985/6). 'The subject of literature', *Cultural Critique,* 2, 95–104.

Eagleton, T. (1993). 'The crisis of contemporary culture', *The New Left Review,* 196, 29–42.

Edwards, T., Fitz, J. and Whitty, G. (1989). *The State and Private Education: an Evaluation of the Assisted Places Scheme*, London, Falmer.

Edwards, T., Gewirtz, S. and Whitty, G. (1992). 'Whose choice of schools? Making sense of city technology colleges', in Arnot, M. and Barton, L. (eds) *Voicing Concerns*, Wallingford, Triangle.

Edwards, T. and Whitty, G. (1990). 'Urban education after the Reform Act', paper presented at the BERA Annual Conference, Roehampton Institute of Higher Education, September.

Evans, J. and Lunt, I. (1990). *Local Management of Schools and Special Educational Needs*, London, University of London Institute of Education.

Evetts, J. (1993). 'LMS and headship: changing contexts for micropolitics', *Educational Review*, 45 (1), 53–66.

Ferris, J. (1985). 'Citizenship and the crisis of the welfare state', in Bean, P., Ferris, J. and Whynes, D. (eds) *In Defence of Welfare*, London, Tavistock.

Fidler, B. and Bowles, G. (eds) (1989). *Effective Local Management of Schools*, London, Longman.

Flew, A. (1991). 'Educational services: independent competition or maintained monopoly', in Green, D. G. (ed.) *Empowering the Parents*, London, Institute of Economic Affairs.

Foucault, M. (1971). *The Order of Discourse*, Paris, Gallimard.

Foucault, M. (1974). *The Order of Things*, London, Tavistock.

Foucault, M. (1977). *The Archeology of Knowledge*, London, Tavistock.

Foucault, M. (1980). *Power/Knowledge: Selected Interviews and Other Writings, 1972–77* (ed. C. Gordon), Brighton, Harvester Press.

Foucault, M. (1981). *The History of Sexuality, Vol.1.* Harmondsworth, Penguin.

Gewirtz, S. and Ozga, J. (1990). 'Partnership, pluralism and education policy', *Journal of Education Policy*, 5 (1), 35–46.

Gewirtz, S., Ball, S. J. and Bowe, R. (1993b). 'Values and ethics in the education market place: the case of Northwark Park', *International Studies in the Sociology of Education*, 3 (2), 233–54.

Gewirtz, S., Ball, S. J. and Bowe, R. (1994). 'Parents, privilege and the education market place', *Research Papers in Education*, 9 (1), 3–30.

Giddens, A. (1987). *Social Theory and Modern Sociology*, Cambridge, Polity Press.

Gintis, H. (1989). 'The power to switch: on the political economy of consumer sovereignty', in Bowles, S., Edwards, R. and Shepard, W. (eds) *Unconventional Wisdom: Essays in Honour of JK Galbraith*, New York, Houghton-Mifflin.

Gipps, C. and Brown, M. (1992). National Assessment in Primary Schools Project, Seminar Paper, Institute of Education, University of London.

Goodchild, S. and Holly, P. (1989). *Management for Change: The Garth Hill Experience*, London, Falmer.

Gutmann, A. (1987). *Democratic Education*, Princeton, NJ, Princeton University Press.

Habermas, J. (1985). 'Neoconservative culture criticism in the United States and West Germany: an intellectual movement in two political cultures', in Bernstein, R. J. (ed.) *Habermas and Modernity*, Cambridge, Polity Press.

Hall, D. (1990). 'The National Curriculum and the two cultures: towards a humanistic perspective', *Geography*, 22 (2), 310–20.

Halpin, D., Power, S. and Fitz, J. (1993). 'Opting into state control? Headteachers and some paradoxes of grant-maintained status', *International Studies in Sociology of Education*, 3 (1), 3–23.

Halsey, A. H., Heath, A. and Ridge, J. (1980). *Origins and Destinations*, Oxford, Clarendon Press.

Handscomb, G. (1992). 'The rhetoric and reality of LMS: a case study of one secondary school', Paper Presented to the 8th ERA Research Network Seminar, 12 February.

Hargreaves, D. and Hopkins, D. (1991). *The Empowered School*, London, Cassell.

Harker, R. and May, S. A. (1993). 'Code and *habitus*: comparing the accounts of Bernstein and Bourdieu', *British Journal of Sociology of Education*, 14 (2), 169–79.

Hart, D. (1990). 'Accelerating pressures and how heads can cope', *School Governor*, September, 40–1.

Harvey, L. (1990). *Critical Social Research*, London, Allen and Unwin.

Hatton, E. (1988). 'Teachers' work as bricolage: implications for teacher education', *British Journal of Sociology of Education*, 14 (2), 169–79.

Hayek, F. (1980). *Individualism and Economic Order*, Chicago, University of Chicago Press.

Heelas, P. and Morris, P. (eds) (1992). *The Values of the Enterprise Culture: the Moral Debate*, London, Routledge.

Hess, A. (1992). *School Restructuring, Chicago Style: a Midway Report*, Chicago, Chicago Panel on Public School Policy and Finance.

Hirsch, E. D. (1987). *Cultural Literacy: What Every American Needs to Know*, Boston, Houghton-Mifflin.

Hirsch, F. (1977). *Social Limits to Growth*, London, Routledge and Kegan Paul.

Hirschmann, A. O. (1970). *Exit, Voice and Loyalty*, Cambridge, MA, Harvard University Press.

HMI (1990a). *Special Needs Issues*, London, HMSO.

HMI (1990b). *Teaching and Learning in the New York City Schools*, London, HMSO.

Hoy, D. (1986). 'Power, repression, progress: Foucault, Lukes and the Frankfurt School' in Hoy, D. (ed.) *Foucault: a Critical Reader*, Oxford, Blackwell.

Huckle, J. and Machon, P. (1990). 'Geography and political education in the National Curriculum', *Teaching Geography*, 15 (2), 53–7.

Jackson, M. (1989). 'CBI struggles to "save" curriculum from Baker', *The Times Educational Supplement*, 24 March, 1.

Jameson, F. (1984). 'Postmodernism or the cultural logic of late capitalism', *New Left Review*, 147, 61–84.

Jenkins, K. and Brickley, P. (1990). 'History and the National Curriculum', *Teaching History*, 62, 10–16.

Jonathan, R. (1990). 'State education service or prisoner's dilemma: the "hidden hand" as source of education policy', *Educational Philosophy and Theory*, 22 (1), 16–24.

Jones, D. M. and Ball, S. J. (1994). 'Michel Foucault and the discourse of education', in MacLaren, P. and Giarelli, J. (eds) *Critical Theory and Educational Research*. Albany, NY, State University of New York Press.

Jones, K. (1989). *Right Turn*, London, Radius.

Keat, R. (1991). 'Starship Britain or universal enterprise', in Keat, R. and Abercrombie, N. (eds) *Enterprise Culture*, London, Routledge.

Kedourie, H. (1988). *Errors and Evils of the New History*, London, Centre for Policy Studies.

Kenway, J. (1990). 'Class, gender and private schooling', in Dawkins, D. (ed.) *Power and Politics in Education*, London, Falmer Press.

Kickert, W. (1991). 'Steering at a distance; a new paradigm of public governance in Dutch higher education', paper for the European Consortium for Political Research, University of Essex, March 1991.

Kingdom, J. (1992). *No Such Thing as Society?*, Buckingham, Open University Press.

Knight, B. (1990). 'Eight years of local financial management', *School Governor*, September, 6–9.

Konstant, D. (1991). 'Catholic schools and market forces', *The Bishops' Conferences, of Great Britain, Briefing*, 21 (20) 24 October, 9–13.

Lee, T. (1991). *Additional Educational Needs and LMS: Methods and Money 1991–2*, Bath, Centre for the Analysis of Social Policy, University of Bath.

Levacic, R. (1982). 'Local management of schools as an organisational form: theory and application', paper to the 8th ERA Research Network Meeting, University of Warwick, February.

Lieberman, A. (1990). *Schools as Collaborative Cultures: Creating the Future Now*, London, Falmer.

Lowery, D., de Hoog, R. and Lyons, W. E. (1992). 'Citizenship in the empowered locality', *Urban Affairs Quarterly*, 28 (1), 69–103.

Lyotard, J.-F. (1984). *The Post-modern Condition: a Report on Knowledge*, Manchester, Manchester University Press.

Mac an Ghaill, M. (1991). 'State school policy: contradictions, confusions and contestation', *Journal of Education Policy*, 6 (3), 299–314.

McLaughlin, R. (1991). 'Can the information systems for the NHS internal market work?', *Public Money and Management*, Autumn, 37–41.

Maguire, M. (1993). Personal communication.

Maguire, M. and Ball, S. J. (1994). Researching politics and the politics of research', *International Journal of Qualitative Studies in Education.*

Mann, D. (1981). 'Education policy analysis and the rent-a-troika business', paper presented at the American Educational Research Association annual meeting, Los Angeles, April.

Marquand, D. (1992). 'The enterprise culture: new wine in old bottles?', in Heelas, P. and Morris, P. (eds) *The Values of the Enterprise Culture: the Moral Debate*, London, Routledge.

Matsaganis, M. and Glennerster, H. (1993). 'Is cream skimming the Achilles heel of fundholding?', paper presented at the School of Advanced Urban Studies Conference on Quasi-markets, University of Bristol 22–24 March.

Metcalfe, L. (1991). 'Public management: from imitation to innovation', paper to European Consortium for Political Research, University of Essex, March.

Minogue, K. (1993). 'Is Conservatism at last developing a theory?', Lecture at King's College London, 16 February.

Moore, D. and Davenport, S. (1990). 'Choice: the new improved sorting machine' in Boyd, W. L. and Walberg, H. J. (eds) *Choice in Education: Potential and Problems*, Berkeley, McCutchan.

Morrell, F. (1989). *Children of the Future*, London, Hogarth Press.

Nagel, T. (1991). *Equality and Partiality*, Oxford, Oxford University Press.

NASSP Bulletin (1991). The challenge of change in reform and restructuring, *NASSP Bulletin*, 75 (537), October.

Offe, C. (1984). *Contradictions of the Welfare State*, London, Hutchinson.

O'Hear, A. (1988). 'The importance of traditional learning', *British Journal of Educational Studies*, 35, 17–29.

O'Hear, A. (1991a). *Father of Child-centredness: John Dewey and the Ideology of Modern Education*, London, Centre for Policy Studies.

O'Hear, A. (1991b). 'Out of sync with Bach', *Times Educational Supplement*, 22 February.

Orfield, G. (1990). 'Do we know anything worth knowing about the educational effects of magnet schools?', in Clune, W. and Witte, J. (eds) *Choice and Control in American Education, Vol. 2*, London, Falmer.

Ozga, J. (1987). 'Studying education policy through the lives of policy makers', in Walker, S. and Barton, L. (eds) *Changing Policies. Changing Teachers*, Milton Keynes, Open University Press.

Ozga, J. (1990). 'Policy research and policy theory: a comment on Fitz and Halpin', *Journal of Education Policy*, 5 (4), 359–62.

Paulu, N. (1989). *Improving Schools and Empowering Parents: Choice in American Education*, Washington, DC, US Government Printing Office.

Petersen, W. O. (1993). 'The value of values: the principal's role', paper presented at the Annual Meeting of the American Educational Research Association, Atlanta, GA.

Plant, R. (1992). 'Enterprise in its place: the moral limits of markets', in

Heelas, P. and Morris, P. (eds) *The Values of the Enterprise Culture: the Moral Debate*, London, Routledge.

Podgorecki, A. (1974). 'Ethical notions and social life: some problems in the measurement of attitudes', *Quality and Quantity*, 8 (3), 267–82.

Pollard, A. (1992). 'Teachers' responses to the reshaping of primary education', in Arnot, M. and Barton, L. (eds) *Voicing Concerns*, Wallingford, Triangle.

Power, S. (1992). 'Researching the impact of education policy: difficulties and discontinuities', *Journal of Education Policy*, 7 (5), 493–500.

Prunty, J. (1985). 'Signposts for a critical educational policy analysis', *Australian Journal of Education*, 29 (2), 133–40.

Raab, C. (1991). 'Education policy and management: contemporary changes in Britain', paper to International Institute of Administrative Sciences, Copenhagen, July.

Rabinow, P. (1986). *The Foucault Reader*, Harmondsworth, Penguin.

Ralston, K. (1990). 'Getting new things done: the work performance of an academic entrepreneur', *International Journal of Qualitative Studies in Education*, 3 (4), 321–34.

Ranson, S. (1990). 'From 1944 to 1988: education, citizenship and democracy', in Flude, M. and Hammer, M. (eds) *The Education Reform Act 1988: Its Origins and Implications*, London, Falmer Press.

Ranson, S. (1993). 'Renewing education for democracy', paper presented at the Institute of Public Policy Research Conference on Education Policy, London, 23–24 March.

Reekie, W. D. (1984). *Market, Entreprenuers and Liberty*, Brighton, Wheatsheaf.

Regan, D. (1990). *City Technology Colleges: Potentials and Perils*, London, Centre for Policy Studies.

Riseborough, G. (1992). 'Primary headship, state policy and the challenge of the 1990s', *Journal of Education Policy*, 8 (2), 123–42.

Rizvi, F. and Kemmis, S. (1987). *Dilemmas of Reform*, Geelong, Deakin Institute for Studies in Education.

Rose, N. (1989). *Governing the Soul*, London, Routledge.

Rosenholtz, S. J. (1985). 'Effective schools: interpreting the evidence', *American Journal of Education*, 93, 352–88.

Rosenholtz, S. J. (1990). 'Educational reform strategies: will they increase teacher commitment?', in Lieberman, A. (ed.) *Schools as Collaborative Cultures*, London, Falmer.

Said, E. (1986). 'Foucault and the imagination of power', in Hoy, D. (ed.) *Foucault: a Critical Reader*, Oxford, Blackwell.

Saltman, R. B. and Von Otter, C. (1992). *Planned Markets and Public Competition*, Buckingham, Open University Press.

Sarason, S. (1971). *The Culture of the School and the Problem of Change*, Boston, Allyn and Bacon.

Saunders, P. (1986). *Social Theory and the Urban Question*, 2nd edn, London, Hutchinson.

Sawicki, J. (1991). *Disciplining Foucault: Feminism, Power and the Body*, New York, Routledge.

Sayers, A. (1992). 'The human impact of the market', in Heelas, P. and Morris, P. (eds) *The Values of the Enterprise Culture: the Moral Debate*, London, Routledge.

Scheurich, J. (1992). 'A postmodernist review of interviewing: dominance, resistance and chaos', *International Journal of Qualitative Studies in Education.*

Schimell, B. (1991). 'LMS: management planning and policy development issues', MA thesis, Education Area, University of Sussex.

Scruton, R. (1991). 'Rock around the classroom', *Sunday Telegraph*, 10 February.

Sheridan, A. (1980). *The Will to Truth*, London, Tavistock.

Shields, R. (1992). *Lifestyle Shopping: the Subject of Consumption*, London, Routledge.

Sikes, P., Measor, L. and Woods, P. (1985). *Teachers' Careers: Crises and Continuities*, London, Falmer Press.

Smart, B. (1986). 'The politics of truth and the problem of hegemony', in Hoy, D. (ed.) *Foucault: a Critical Reader*, Oxford, Blackwell.

Smyth, J. (ed.) (1993). *A Socially Critical View of the Self-managing School*, London, Falmer.

Spybey, T. (1984). 'Traditional and professional frames of meaning for managers', *Sociology*, 18 (4), 550–62.

Steinfels, P. (1979). *The Neo-conservatives*, New York, The Free Press.

Storey, J. (1983). *Managerial Prerogative and the Question of Control*, London, Routledge.

Therborn, G. (1978). *What Does the Ruling Class Do When It Rules?*, London, New Left Books.

Thomas, H. (1992). 'School goverance and the limits of self-interest', *Educational Review*, 44 (3), 327–33.

Thomas, J. (1993). *Doing Critical Ethnography*, Newbury Park, CA, Sage.

Thurow, L. and Douglas, R. (1972). 'The American distribution of income: a structural problem', US Congress, Joint Economic Committee, Washington, DC.

Tiebout, C. (1956). 'A pure theory of local expenditure', *Journal of Political Economy*, 64 (4), 416–24.

Troman, G. (1989). 'Testing tensions: the politics of educational assessment', *British Education Research Journal*, 15 (3), 279–96.

Trotman, J. and Robertson, S. (1992). 'Taking the Queen's shilling: public policy, research and academics in the 1980s', *Discourse*, 13 (1), 67–89.

Troyna, B. (1992). ' "The hub" and "the Rim": how LMS buckles antiracist education', paper presented at the 8th ERA Research Network Seminar, 12 February.

Troyna, B. (1993). 'Critical social research and education policy', paper presented to the Conference on New Directions in Education Policy Sociology', 30–31 March.

Vincent, C. (1993). 'Community participation? The establishment of city's Parents' Centre', British Educational Research Journal, 19 (3), 227–41.

Walford, G. (1993). 'Self-managing schools, choice and equity', in Smyth, J. (ed.) A Socially Critical View of the Self-managing School, London, Falmer.

Walker, A. (1981). 'Social policy, social administration and the social construction of welfare', Sociology, 15 (2), 255–69.

Wallace, M. (1988). 'Innovation for all: management development in small primary schools', Education Management and Administration, 16 (1), 15–24.

Wallace, M. (1991). 'School development plans: a key to the management of ERA?', paper presented to the 7th ERA Research Network Seminar, 7 February.

Weeres, J. G. and Cooper, B. (1991). 'Public choice perspectives on urban schools', Journal of Education Policy, 6 (5), 57–70.

Weiss, M. (1993). 'New guiding conceptions in the education policy of Germany', Journal of Education Policy, 8 (4), 307–20.

Wexler, P. and Grabiner, G. (1986). 'America during the crisis', in Sharp, R. (ed.) Capitalism, Crisis and Schooling, South Melbourne, Macmillan.

Whitty, G. (1989). 'The New Right and the National Curriculum: state control and market forces', Journal of Education Policy, 4 (4), 329–42.

Whitty, G. (1990). 'The New Right and the National Curriculum: state control of market forces'. In Flude, M. and Hammer, M. (eds) The Education Reform Act 1988: Its Origins and Implications, London, Falmer Press.

Whitty, G. (1991). 'Making sense of urban education after Thatcher', seminar paper, University of Liverpool, Department of Education, 1 May.

Whitty, G. et al. (1989). 'Assisting whom? Benefits and costs of the assisted places scheme', in Hargreaves, A. and Reynolds, D. (ed.) Educational Policies: Controversies and Critiques, London, Falmer.

Widgery, D. (1988). The National Health Service: a Radical Perspective, London, Hogarth.

Willetts, D. (1992). Modern Conservativism, London, Penguin.

Williamson, O. E. (1975). Markets and Hierarchies: Analysis and Anti-trust Implications, New York, The Free Press.

Willis, P. (1976). Learning to Labour, Aldershot, Gower.

Witte, J. (1993). 'The Milwaukee Parental Choice Program: the first thirty months', paper delivered at the American Educational Research Association Annual Meeting, Atlanta, GA, 15–18 April.

Woods, P. (1992). 'Empowerment through choice? Towards an understanding of parental choice and school responsiveness', Education Management and Administration, 20 (4), 204–11.

Yeatman, A. (1993). 'Corporate managerialism and the shift from the welfare to the competition state', Discourse, 13 (2), 10–17.

Index